Selected books by Jeffries Wyman:

Binding and Linkage: Functional Chemistry of Biological Macromolecules,
coauthored by Stanley J. Gill
(University Science Books, 1990)
Available at www.BarnesandNoble.com

Letters from Japan
(Protean Press, 2010)
Available at www.ProteanPress.com

Alaska Journal
(Protean Press, 2010)
Available at www.ProteanPress.com

In addition to his classic 1965 paper with Monod and Changeux ("On the Nature of Allosteric Transitions," *Journal of Molecular Biology*) and other articles published throughout his career, Jeffries Wyman's scientific correspondence and other papers are preserved in the Harvard University Archives and the Service des Archives in the Institut Pasteur.

KIPLING'S CAT
A Memoir of My Father

Jeffries Wyman speaking to colleagues in Italy in 1981.
(Photographer unknown. Reprinted, with permission, from the Annual Review of
Biophysics, *Volume 16 © 1987 by Annual Reviews www.annualreviews.org and by
permission of Jane Gill Kellenberger.)*

KIPLING'S CAT
A Memoir of My Father

Anne Cabot Wyman

PROTEAN PRESS
Rockport, Massachusetts

OPEN BOOK SYSTEMS, INC. / PROTEAN PRESS
37-J Whistlestop Mall
Rockport, MA 01966
www.ProteanPress.com

14 13 12 11 10   1 2 3 4 5

First Edition 2010

Library of Congress Cataloging-in-Publication Data
Wyman, Anne Cabot.
  Kipling's cat : a memoir of my father / by Anne Cabot Wyman. — 1st ed.
    p. cm.
  Includes index.
  ISBN 978-0-9625780-4-5
  1. Wyman, Jeffries, 1901-1995. 2. Wyman, Anne Cabot—Family. 3. Fathers and daughters—United States. 4. Scientists—United States—Biography. 5. Diplomats—United States—Biography 6. Painters—United States—Biography. 7. Adventure and adventurers—United States—Biography. 8. Eccentrics and eccentricities—United States—Biography 9. Upper class—Massachusetts—Boston—Biography. I. Title.
  CT275.W895W96 2010
  974.4´ 61044092—dc22
  [B]
                                                                  2009038193

MANUFACTURED IN THE UNITED STATES OF AMERICA

CREDITS

For my brothers, Jeff and Dimitri

And with special thanks
to my old Globe *colleague,*
Jerry Ackerman

Contents

Contents

Introduction
Kipling's Cat

Whenever I think of my father, he reminds me of the clever, vanishing cat in Rudyard Kipling's "The Cat that Walked by Himself," part of his 1902 collection for children, *Just So Stories*.

Of all the animals that came to the Cave Woman for shelter and food, only the Cat refused to become her servant, reserving the right to roam. "He will kill mice," Kipling writes, "and he will be kind to Babies when he is in the house, just as long as they do not pull his tail too hard. But when he has done that, and between times, and when the moon gets up and night comes, he is the Cat that walks by himself, and all places are alike to him. Then he goes out to the Wet Wild Woods or up the Wet Wild Trees or on the Wet Wild Roofs, waving his wild tail and walking by his wild lone."

My father was just like that.

KIPLING'S CAT
A Memoir of My Father

Chapter 1

Blood Ties

Two days after my father died in Paris, I flew over from Boston and went into the darkened room where his body was laid out on the bed. A candle burned on the bureau. The medicines he took for Parkinson's stood on the mantel, jumbled with bronze and ivory figures brought back from his travels. Against the hectic red and green wallpaper he'd chosen himself hung bold watercolors he'd painted in Europe. I reached out and put my hand on his forehead. It was cold and the skin didn't move on the bone.

What a contrast to the vigorous life I remembered! I thought back to a summer evening in Brookline when I was nine. The sky was violet over the grassy hill behind our house. Cicadas were tuning up in the trees. My father's little Ford Model-A roadster crunched over the gravel, its open rumble seat clinking with five-gallon jars filled with blue liquid. It was the blood of horseshoe crabs, brought from Woods Hole for an experiment Father was doing at Harvard. My younger brother and I climbed onto the back of the Ford to see. Blue blood, like "bluebloods" from the aristocracy? No, naturally blue blood from one of Earth's prehistoric survivors, Father explained. Copper in the blood of horseshoe crabs makes it blue. It has special properties. The blood contains an ingredient called *limulus amoebocyte lysate*, which doctors still use today to ensure that medical devices and drugs are free of bacteria.

Blood marked a lifelong preoccupation for Father. At the age of seventy-five, his obsession with the big hemoglobin molecule, which carries oxygen to the body and removes carbon dioxide, took him to the Amazon on an expedition to learn why even red fish blood, in those seasonally oxygen-poor waters, behaved so differently from the red blood cells of humans. And his book on the regulatory mechanism of binding and linkage in the heme protein was published the year he turned ninety.

But if blood was his scientific love, family ties and blood relations were also a perpetual interest. We lived with the legacy of ancestors who had known each other in Boston's small Brahmin world, a world of so-called "bluebloods." Our little household of four was entwined with grandparents, uncles and aunts and rafts of cousins. The generations met every year at big family parties and in old summer enclaves in Maine or on Cape Cod. In the winter, colonies of relatives clustered in the upscale Boston suburbs of Brookline or Dover or Milton. The men worked together in offices on State Street in downtown Boston or in labs at Harvard. Their wives belonged to "Mothers' Clubs." They were all considered—and considered themselves—True Bostonians.

Father had a sister, eight years older than he, but he was brought up as an only child and, when he married my mother, Anne Cabot, he moved happily into a huge clan of Cabots, Forbeses and Paines. Years later his letters recited visits from nephews, nieces and cousins wherever he was. A great-nephew recently told me of once going to see Father in Paris and being so charmed that he took notes of their conversation. Father's correspondence with me included a lengthy discussion about which member of the family should manage his money.

My mother's four older brothers lived in Dover; her younger sister raised her family in Cambridge. My parents stayed close to my grandmother Cabot in Brookline, building a house next door to hers. On the top of our hill were a Cabot great-aunt and her husband, Robert Treat Paine. One of their five sons, Richard, lived beyond them in the house where my mother grew up, before her father, Henry B. Cabot, built his own Victorian house with its distant view over the Massachusetts State House to Boston Harbor.

When my brother, Jeffy, and I were little we would wait daily for Father's return home from his Harvard lab, which meant tea time. Then we would follow our parents through a grove of pines and bittersweet to the tennis court where, every evening in summer, they met Richard Paine for a threesome game. In winter, my parents and Cousin Richard played squash in the court attached to his parents' garage.

Then, while we children were served supper downstairs, Father and Mother would bathe, taking turns using the bathwater as though they had grown up in a desert. Afterward they would change into their evening clothes and come down to read aloud to us before we were sent up to bed. It was a family joke that Father read Sir Walter Scott like the Bible and the Bible like some racy novel. My favorite was *Pilgrim's Progress*, with its strange illustrations and tales of "the Slough of Despond," encounters with "Mr. Worldly Wiseman" and battles with the ghastly "Apollyon" on Christian's road to "the Celestial City."

As the light faded, Father would sit in the red Morris chair with his back to the French windows. Mother, on the other side of the fireplace, would be knitting or sewing or perhaps holding one of us on her lap. He smoked a pipe and so, quite often, did she. The library walls were covered with China-trade tea paper except for a wall of books behind the small sofa. A special panel of raised paper with birds and chrysanthemums was glued over the fireplace. Mother's long dinner dress would often be something she had created from old damask curtains. Father wore a black velvet smoking jacket and evening slippers. He had one red pair of slippers and one green pair, both of which were used for occasional spankings. Once, when Jeffy was due to be punished, he begged, "Not the red slippers, Father. Please not the red slippers," as though the color made all the difference.

My brother's room was at the east end of the house and my room was next to his. Then came the nursery, which had a coal grate and an upright piano on which our young Irish cook played "Red Sails in the Sunset." Then the stairs and, at the far end of the house, our parents' sitting room, bathroom and tiny cold bedroom, just big enough for two end tables and their double sleigh bed. Perhaps the smallness saved heat.

I sometimes had nightmares. The gardener's dog, Mr. Rex, was biting my fingernails or someone was climbing in over the windowsill. Father would come into my room and recite the Lord's Prayer, in Greek, to comfort me. "Did you know someone once wrote that prayer on the head of a pin?" he would ask. Later on I took two years of Greek; I remember nothing except the start of each chapter of Xenophon's *Anabasis*, "And the next day they set forth . . ." That idea of a string of new days formed a central part of my father's philosophy. He did not deny his own past but refused to be worried or tied down by it.

All of this changed when my mother died of Hodgkin's lymphoma in 1943. Like the cat in Rudyard Kipling's *Just So Stories*, Father vanished into "the Wet Wild Woods, waving his wild tail and walking by his wild lone." Within months, he left Jeffy and me with Mother's oldest brother and went off to work for the Navy. When his short second marriage failed in 1949, he moved out to Milton and then on to Alaska, Japan and Paris. One night in Rome in 1954, when Father had been alerted that two FBI men wanted to question him about his friend J. Robert Oppenheimer, he went back to sleep and the next day, after the inquisition, kept a luncheon appointment. If Jeff or I wrote to him in a state of gloom, he would reply, "I am sorry that you are so down but, by the time this reaches you, I am sure you will be feeling differently."

His thoughts often took a whimsical turn. One Easter, he wrote me from Europe, "I shall be 73 in June and I begin to realize that various parts of my body are wearing out . . . But it would be awful if people were to live forever! If I can go on long enough to see how things are developing in the next 15 years, I shall be content, whether or not I like what happens." Then his letter turned to the holy occasion.

"Did it ever occur to you," he wrote, "that the whole of Christian faith is based on the ritual of cannibalism, the Mass being the central feature? This is not in any way to denigrate it," the letter continued. "As I understand it, ritual cannibalism was an almost immemorial and fundamental part of human culture all over the world in prehistoric days. It still survives, as I saw it, in New Guinea and many other primitive places. But now it has been sublimated, without being really hidden, in the church."

I reread that statement as I was nearing the age my father was when he wrote it. It struck me as incredibly funny, coming out of the blue on the day conventionally devoted to celebrating the resurrection of Christ and the immortality of the human spirit. Then I was struck by the candor and open-mindedness of the thought. Cannibalism, certainly. What else is the Eucharist? My father's deadpan reflection was absurd in its context and in the pomposity of its presentation. But for me there was also nobility in the reach and unexpectedness of his vision.

I remember Father becoming equally engaged when I spent a morning, at the age of about eight, trying to catch sunlight in a shoebox. He and Jeffy struggled with the notion that "tomorrow" will be yesterday, two days from now. And he would describe, with enchantment, Jeffy's invitation to visit his club in an old stone tower on the hill. Father recalled asking "who are the other members?" and Jeffy's proud reply that he was "the only member" of the club.

There were years when we were apart, even years when we were estranged, but my father stayed in touch through long letters, which he wrote by hand on thin paper and often in pencil. Usually the letters only told of his "doings," with asides to please make sure that moths and mildew weren't attacking his treasures at home. It was often unclear in the letters where he was. He wrote little about his work, which he rightly feared we would not understand. Instead he included detailed accounts of museums and native villages, finding each work of art "the most beautiful of its kind," and each aboriginal encounter "the most welcoming." His advice, when he felt compelled to give it, could be devastatingly off the mark. His insights about marriage and the impact that two stepmothers had on Jeffy and me were limited.

In the end, again like Kipling's Cat, Father left us behind. Sometimes he would be by your side; the next moment he would be gone in mind, body or spirit. Father could draw blood but he was more fun than anyone I have ever known. I want to follow his trail, find out who he was and understand how he shaped my life.

Chapter 2

Paying the Fare to the Moon

W/e scarcely knew my father's parents. His mother, Helen Mackey, died in 1921, when Father was halfway through college. My grandfather, the second Jeffries in the Wyman line, lived on and remarried, but Father seldom spoke of him. We saw him just once a year on Christmas at his fusty little house off Follen Street in Cambridge. Somehow I always felt that my father adored his mother but was ashamed of his father, who had become jobless and alcoholic when he was forty. That shame seemed unfair and, while my grandmother appeared safely lodged in Father's memory, I always wanted to know more about my disfavored grandfather.

Most of my knowledge about Grandpa Wyman comes from his diaries and the photographs he took so lovingly. In the black-and-white image that now hangs on my bathroom wall, a toddler in a white dress balances on a sandy beach, held up by his mother. He looks at the footing ahead and she, in her encompassing black bathing suit, looks down at him. The next photo shows an unsmiling tot in wide striped pants and a squashy white hat, perched on his father's knee. The father's left arm is around the boy's back while his right hand, fingers spread, touches the child's knee as though it were

*My father with his father,
1903. (Photographed by
Helen Mackey; collection of
the author.)*

made of glass. The date is 1903; my father was two and the place was
their summer house in East Gloucester.

The same collection shows a photo of Father, by now perhaps
thirteen, sitting on the porch steps with a telescope across his knees.
He's wearing light-colored knickers and a soft hat. There are dark
circles under his eyes, which seems strange. But the long fingers and
the pose of his hands, even then, are familiar to me. One of the
Gloucester neighbors was Mr. Wonson—"an ancient mariner who
had sailed into the Golden Gate when there were no houses along
the shore," my father told me. Another neighbor was a retired minister, Mr. Caulkins, who is shown in a photo with feet stretched out on
a canvas deck chair, teaching my father Greek at the age of perhaps
fifteen. The inquiring mind is already visible.

Like his father, my father was essentially an only child. His sister,
Helen, was eight years older and seems to have been anxious to leave
home early. After graduating from Smith College, Helen stayed in
western Massachusetts to work for the *Springfield Republican*, where
she met and married Duncan Aikman. Also a journalist, Aikman

Jeffries, at age thirteen or so, already has an eye on science. (Photographer unknown; collection of the author.)

had worked as a correspondent in Europe during World War I and had contracted the flu, which turned into tuberculosis and required convalescence at Saranac in upstate New York. Soon after their marriage, Helen and Duncan moved to El Paso, where their three children were born. Jobs with the *Los Angeles Times* and later the *New York Times* kept the family away from New England, though I remember one Christmas visit in Brookline and another on Cape Cod. Our Aikman cousins seemed much more sophisticated than we. The oldest, Cicely, wore lipstick and powder.

Father's parents wintered in Wellesley, Massachusetts, and summered on the North Shore. There were few relatives: two great-aunts, who were like surrogate parents to my grandfather, or remote cousins, like the person my father would later refer to as "Squire Williams," who lived in Northborough. It seems likely that Father had never known him at all. He would have heard of these people from my grandfather, who had almost no family of his own and therefore, perhaps, cared deeply about who was who and passed on that genealogical preoccupation.

In his old age, my father spoke of these citizens and talked of their relationship to Boston history and to each other. But we never saw any of those Wyman relatives. And, when Father's second wife, Rosamond Forbes, heard of some Wyman cousins living on Beacon Hill, he dissuaded her from going to call on them. When it came to his own family, it was the heritage that counted, not the surviving heirs. It was a heritage that was old and rich in willpower, Puritan values and a strong sense of purpose.

So much of our own family lore centered around the Cabots that I was surprised to learn that my father's American lineage was older, if less prosperous, than my mother's. By the time the Cabots got to Salem from the island of Jersey in 1770, the Wyman progenitors, Francis and John, had already been in Woburn for 130 years, started a tannery and built a homestead that still stands. Four generations later, in 1778, Zebadiah Wyman and his second cousin Eunice produced a first son named Rufus.

My father's scientific bent began with this slender bony-faced man, who became a doctor and, in 1818, the first medical superintendent of the McLean Hospital for the Insane, then being created in Charlestown by physicians at the Massachusetts General Hospital. Based on his surveys of similar institutions, Rufus decreed that his asylum should have such features as washable rooms, under-floor heating and "airing courts" where the patients could get out of doors. More important, Rufus recognized that his "boarders" needed kindness, time and a regular routine in order to recover.

By the time Rufus resigned in 1835, the asylum had treated some 1,200 patients. Roughly half had been released and, of these, more than half were considered cured. One patient, believed possessed of the devil and whipped at home, went on to make a small fortune as a peddler. In seventeen years, Rufus was absent from the hospital a total of five nights. His yearly salary over that time escalated to $1,500, and he received a bonus of $1,000 when he left McLean to build a house on Warren Street in Roxbury, where he lived with his wife and two of his five children until his death at the age of sixty-four in 1842. A bronze plaque of him hangs in the vestibule of Boston's Museum of Science.

Rufus's third son, my father's grandfather, had the family looks and disposition. Named after Rufus's patron, Dr. John Jeffries, who had once left his Boston medical practice to cross the English Channel in a balloon, the first Jeffries Wyman was an anatomist. Among his claims to fame was his identification of the gorilla as a "new" species of ape, a feat he performed in 1847 by studying bones brought back from Africa. Two years later, his forensic skills were called on to identify the charred bones of Dr. George Parkman, who had been murdered by a Harvard chemistry professor, John W. Webster, over an unpaid debt.

Like Rufus, the first Jeffries Wyman had a medical degree, but my great-grandfather soon abandoned medicine for academia. In 1847, at the age of thirty-three, he was named Hersey Professor of Anatomy at Harvard. Nineteen years later he was appointed director of Harvard's brand-new Peabody Museum. He was also a founder of the National Academy of Sciences, a president of the Boston Society of Natural History and the first curator of the Lowell Institute. He was praised by a biographer for avoiding controversy. But he was bold enough to speak against his friend, the naturalist Louis Agassiz, in a dispute with a fellow anatomist, Asa Gray, over Charles Darwin's theory of evolution. Agassiz didn't buy Darwin's ideas; Gray (and my great-grandfather) did. And when his mulatto janitor, Clary, was recruited for the Civil War on the salary of a laborer rather than that of a soldier, my great-grandfather wrote to the U.S. Army Paymaster, stating that the policy "puts the government in a very shabby light; its members are disgracing themselves in the eyes of the world."

In 1874 my great-grandfather wrote a scholarly paper titled "Cannibalism among the American Aborigines," in which he concluded from Indian shell-heaps in Florida that the practice was quite likely. He wryly noted that "not only is human flesh reported to taste good, but also the victor in a tribal war may believe that if he eats [a vanquished enemy] in this life he makes sure of it that there will be no trouble with him in the hereafter, for he possesses him body and soul already."

My grandfather, the second Jeffries, must have been different in every respect from his eminent father and grandfather. Unlike his lean forebears, Grandpa was shaped like Humpty Dumpty and dressed like him too, in a black cloth suit and tie. He was the only child of his father's second marriage and his mother, Annie Williams, died of typhoid the year my grandfather was born. His father, the anatomist, died when my grandfather was ten, leaving Grandpa in Cambridge with his step-aunt, Alice Wheelwright, and two older half-sisters, Susie and Molly. Even before his death, though, my great-grandfather had been an absent parent. Because he'd had tuberculosis, he was advised not to see his son. Besides, his work among the Indian shell-heaps kept him in Florida for most of the winter months. They kept in touch through correspondence, as my absent father kept in touch with us almost a century later. The admonitory tone of the parental letters is similar to my father's, too. "If you do not behave well," my great-grandfather wrote to his five-year-old son, "you must recollect that you will be punished in some way." Then the father added, "You have printed the letters very well and if you try to make some every day you will soon learn to write."

┅

And Grandpa, like many others of his time and like my father afterwards, did write all the time, keeping track of his own life as though it would not exist otherwise. His youthful diaries were full of anxiety and yearning. Flipping through unfilled pages for 1882 when he was eighteen, my grandfather glumly wrote, "I wonder what I shall be doing . . . Whether I shall be alive and, if so, whether I shall be in business or in school & whether I shall be well and happy." On the day he caught up with this entry my grandfather noted that he had gone for a long ride on his bicycle and wished he could go to see a friend off for the West. "I am afraid he is mad with me," he wrote of the departing chum.

Later the same year he wrote, "After tea, went and got Max [Louis Agassiz's son] & I am ashamed to write it but we went to Boston to a whore house [those last two words are crossed out] & I went to bed with a girl. I am disgraced for life." The entry was marked "Private to be read by no one. Burn rather than read." This frequent refrain, I think, shows how desperately Grandpa Wyman longed for a confidant.

Nine days later Grandpa started his first job, working on the Chicago, Burlington and Quincy Railroad for its founder, John Murray Forbes, a friend and admirer of my great-grandfather's. The high point of my grandfather's life, as Father remembered it, came when he drove a train through a line of striking railroad workers in Alliance, Nebraska. For Grandpa, it must have been a great act of managerial responsibility. But the family in Cambridge did not approve of his becoming a scab and told him to come home. Once back, he married Helen Mackey and got a job with John Murray's oldest son, William Hathaway Forbes, as a vice-president of the Bell Telephone Company in Boston. It was never clear what his job entailed but he quit that post in 1904, when he was just forty. His working life had lasted twenty-two years.

This history cast long shadows over my father's childhood. "My mother thought Grandpa's retirement was a tragic thing," Father told me late in his own life. Apparently it was, for, though my grandfather continued to go to Boston to check on his investments, he began drinking heavily. My father remembered Grandpa lumbering onto the Wellesley trolley at eleven o'clock one morning and asking loudly, "Where do we pay the fare to the moon?"

"Imagine how I shrank," Father recalled. "The whole streetcar heard him." Then Father added, surprisingly, that the drinking "was worse for Aunt Helen, because a girl was more a captive of her environment." But, as I listened to the story, I admired my grandfather for his poetic query, and imagined the driver laughing as he recited it to his wife when he got home that night.

With his sister Helen gone, Father found himself alone with his parents. "My high school years in Wellesley were the worst," he told me. "My father was drinking and I had only one friend." Did Father realize he was reenacting his own father's days of misery as he and his only pal spent the afternoons rambling through the countryside or sometimes bicycling from Cambridge to Weston to visit acquaintances?

If my father kept any record of those years, it has been lost. But Grandpa Wyman's diary for the year Father was ten is an enumeration of trivia: daily trips to "the safes and Kidder Peabody," his investment manager; trips to the library where Grandpa borrowed books about Willard clocks; visits from his Aunt Alice and half-sisters Susie and Molly; details about the weather and the cost of such items as a ton of furnace coal ($7.00), a "Brussels rug" for Helen's room ($12.00) or "a framed picture of President Eliot of Harvard" ($5.00). Each day seemed to end with "a stop to see Mr. Thwing," who, I presume, kept a tavern.

Again from the 1911 diary: My grandfather sent his daughter Helen a check for $2.00 on her birthday, then spent a month with his wife and son at the Shattuck Inn in East Jaffrey, New Hampshire. The parents went out for walks while their son skated, snowshoed or skied on new skis that were bought at his request and delivered to him at the inn. There is no record of Father's progress on them. But among many clippings about marriages and deaths glued into the diary there are accounts of a fire in the Hoosac railroad tunnel and of Roald Amundsen's arrival at the South Pole on December 14, 1910.

Today I imagine that Grandpa's preoccupation with clocks reflected a sense that, for him, time had stopped. And his interest in Amundsen and others, of whom he knew only distantly, suggests that his own life had lost the possibility of zest and adventure.

···

I discussed this with Father in his Paris apartment years later, when he himself was chair-bound with Parkinson's disease. He recalled that his father "distinctly had the psychology of someone who'd dropped out. We had practically no company at the house. But," he added, "I can't remember his drinking when invited company was present. And he showed his best side in letters he wrote to close friends."

Father told me his parents "quarreled perpetually"—about details often related to drink or their son, I assume. And indeed his mother's diary for 1921 shows her impatience with her husband. "Jeff is sick with a bad cold," she wrote on April 23. "He is almost unbearable at times and has no control over his nerves." The family was moving that year and the sale of household belongings was a constant concern. Yet, after they sold the Wellesley property in April, they went to the inn in Jaffrey before removing to Cambridge.

"We weren't poor," Father remembered, "just very limited. My father made no money but, to his credit, he had accumulated enough money to live on." Here, perhaps, lie the roots of my father's compulsive frugality.

As we talked that morning, some seventy years after his mother's death, I asked Father if it were true that he loved his mother but hated his father.

"No," Father said. "I think he probably had much deeper feelings than my mother." Recalling the past, Father sighed and folded his hands in the big armchair. "He used to go sailing with me very often. He was not a good sailor. But I think he doted on me, so he went along." I could imagine Grandpa Wyman, shaped like a sack in his black serge suit, huddled under the swinging boom of the small boat, while my lean agile father showed off his prowess at the tiller.

What were my grandfather's strong points, I asked. "He had a most pungent way of speaking," Father said. "He was quite a good phrase-maker and made pointed and striking characterizations of people. Although he had somewhat repudiated his family, he was very proud of it. And he was proud that I'd made such good contacts with my classmates in college—Will Forbes, for example," he added. Will was the grandson of Grandpa's benefactor at the telephone company.

Had Grandpa been religious, I asked. I was thinking of Father's own intellectual approach to theology, and of an entry in Grandpa's diary reporting that my grandmother believed going to church would do her good. Next to that entry Grandpa had scrawled, "Not a damn bit of it." Father's answer was definite. "No," he said. "He never went to church."

And what were my grandfather's interests? "He was a big eater," Father said, then went on to recall that his father had often talked about his time with the railroad in the West, where he had seen Indians. "Nebraska was a wild place in those days." My father's tone gave me a sense of his father's heartbreak and longing for freedom and for the romantic Wild West. And I remembered the sad entries of the dutiful boy in my grandfather's early diaries.

Even my grandmother's passing references to her husband made him sound gentle. The year of their move to Cambridge she wrote in her diary, "Jeff packed all morning." And some weeks later, on June 2, "Jeff put up curtains in the passage and dining room." Eleven days later, "After dinner Jeff painted the big clock and put up the netting in the little room window." Clearly Grandpa was making work out of idleness, trying to be helpful. By 1921, my father was an undergraduate at Harvard and his Aunt Molly had sponsored a summer in Europe for him. "Jeff has gone to Boston to say goodbye to dear Jeffries who leaves tomorrow," my grandmother wrote. And a few days after my father had gone, she noted that her grieving husband and the handyman had carved a window box "for Jeffries."

If my grandmother's feelings about her husband were mixed, her diary of 1921 makes it clear that she, too, adored her son. There are constant references to his comings and goings, to tea and long walks together, to reading aloud in the evening, to making "a little tea cake" together one morning, to his departure for college with "no overcoat." And, when my father left for a summer abroad with a friend, she wrote, "I did not go to see him off as I felt quite broken up." Fat, lame and perhaps diabetic, she was unable to face the emotional parting.

It must have been a strange household, full of tension and disappointment. Sometime later that year my grandmother died. I know nothing about it. While I have some dozen years of Grandpa's diaries, I have only one volume from my Wyman grandmother. Perhaps I took her for granted. I had to check that her maiden name Mackey was spelled correctly. Late in his own life Father told me that his great-grandfather "owned ships that went to the Far East . . . [but] he lost a good deal of his money in the panic of the 1870s." Father's Mackey grandfather, William, he said, "lived for a while in Newport, Rhode Island, where my mother was born. Then he took his large family for a time first to France and then to England." Were they connected to the famous shipbuilder, Donald McKay? I think I would have heard if they were.

My father's mother had no special interests that I know of. Her life seemed to consist of putting up with her husband, small social visits and doting upon her son. But my father always spoke of missing her. And, under my grandmother's entry for July 4, 1921, my grandfather had written, "Eight years later and I am all alone—Dear Helen." Was that self-pity or genuine sadness?

That morning in Paris my father told me that his father "was miserable." He felt that Grandpa Wyman had inherited "the apostasy" of an ancestor who backed the South in the Civil War. Like that ancestor, Stephen Whitney, Father said, his own father had "rejected the natural grouping of his fellow Northerners, imagined he was viewed with contempt, and felt very bitter."

Looking back, it seems to me that, from his earliest days as a real orphan, someone who lacked the looks and great brains of his forebears or the wealth of his benefactors, my grandfather felt like an intellectual and social outsider. My grandmother, too, must have felt distressed and alone. Between them, they must have believed that my father, their son, could redeem them.

In contrast, my father's childhood may have been lonely and isolated but he knew he was loved, indeed I think fought over, by both his parents. Neither of them was able to "pay the fare to the moon," but Father, with their affection, and with the genes of Rufus and Jeffries, was ready to set forth and try.

Chapter 3

A World of Ideas

In his Harvard class photo my father is looking straight into the camera without a smile. His eyes are large under faint eyebrows; his nose falls in a plumb-line toward a wide mouth that seems to hide a bunch of snaggly teeth. This is a later version of the little boy in a squashy hat perched on his father's knee, a later version of the youth in a Norfolk jacket and knickers sitting on a porch step with a telescope. But there are traces there already of the young man who would graduate in 1923 with a *summa* in philosophy and a *magna* in biology.

Father was eager to enter a world of new friends and new ideas after his years as a prep school day student at Noble and Greenough in Boston. College was "the best time of my life," he once told me. "I had been miserable at school where I had only one close friend. Now everything was opening up all around me."

His Harvard years, 1919 to 1923, were tempestuous times in the world—years marked by famine abroad, strikes at home, the inauguration of the ill-fated League of Nations, the scandal-plagued administration of President Warren G. Harding, the Sacco and Vanzetti trial, the first transatlantic crossings by air, the publication

Jeffries in 1919, the year he launched his scholarly career at Harvard, photographed by his father. (Collection of the author.)

of James Joyce's *Ulysses* and the beginning of America's "great experiment" with prohibition. Then no one had laptop computers or cell phones; few students had cars. But judging by his recollections, Father was happily ensconced in his ivory tower and was paying little attention to such world events. Instead, it seems mostly by chance, he was cultivating friendships that over the years would prove lasting and provide him with pathways to far corners of society and the world.

At Harvard he had rooms in Winthrop House, where he shared an entry with John Tileston Edsall, son of the dean of Harvard's Medical School and a graduate of Milton Academy. Edsall majored in chemistry while Father elected to study philosophy. But a mutual interest in science kindled a lifelong friendship, and Father added biology to his field of concentration. Two decades later, around 1940, they became joint teaching assistants for Harvard's preeminent pioneer in biochemistry, Lawrence J. Henderson. Eventually they taught Henderson's Chemistry 15 course themselves. Much later, in 1958, they co-wrote a textbook which, perhaps presciently, they titled *Biophysical Chemistry, Volume One*. But biophysical science was changing so quickly that there never was a Volume Two.

By the end of their lives their core interests had diverged. My father had moved into theoretical research while Edsall became a political activist and historian of science. Father traveled throughout his life, while Edsall stayed at home. But still they kept in touch, writing, telephoning and visiting whenever possible. After my father's death, Edsall bequeathed their long correspondence to Harvard's archives.

I saw John Edsall regularly until his death in 2002 and his memories were vivid to the last. As undergraduates, he remembered, students occupied suites, each usually with two bedrooms and a central living room. There was a working fireplace but it was rarely used. Meals were provided by the college, and an Irish maid, called a "goodie," came to clean the undergraduates' rooms several times a week. Edsall remembered Father joyously repeating a militant song he overheard the woman sing, which gives some tenor of the times:

> *May the gods above*
> *Send down a dove*
> *With wings as sharp as razors*
> *To cut the throats of the Black and Tans*
> *Who murdered the good Sinn Feiners.*

My father shared a room with Chester Duryea from New York. Duryea's father had murdered his own father when Chester was

Jeffries Wyman with John Edsall, his lifelong friend, at Anne's home in Cambridge, Massachusetts—around 1978. (Author photo.)

about fourteen, Edsall told me. This astonishing fact, while known, apparently was never discussed. Edsall found Father and Duryea "a rather strange combination," and remembered that they kept two goldfish in a bowl, one named Immanuel Kant and the other Rabindranath Tagore. "I don't think they knew which fish was which," Edsall said. Duryea went into business upon graduation but soon quit and withdrew to Tahiti, from where he wrote Father and Edsall long, rambling letters over the years. Another close friend was Carl Weyerhaeuser, whose grandfather was founder of what became the Weyerhaeuser Timber Company. Father visited the Weyerhaeuser mansion in Minnesota and went with Carl on a bicycling trip in Europe in 1921. When I met him at his home in Milton in the 1960s, Weyerhaeuser had five grown children and a small museum of art objects in Duxbury, and he seemed to be somewhat of a mystic.

At the same time, Father was also expanding his Boston connections, through encounters with classmates William Hathaway Forbes, whose grandfather had been my Wyman grandfather's benefactor at the Bell Telephone Company, and John Malcolm Forbes, an early psychologist at the Judge Baker Clinic in Boston who was later one of the original underwriters of Black Mountain College, near Asheville, North Carolina. The Forbeses were cousins and both lived in Milton and summered on Naushon Island off Cape Cod, but they had rather separate circles of friends. Mac drowned while fishing off Naushon in 1941, but Will Forbes, who was my mother's first cousin, became another lifelong chum.

Most of his colleagues, though, were involved in science. Besides Edsall, they included Alfred Mirsky and M.L. "Tim" Anson, both of whom would become preeminent in biological science. Marshall Stone, who became a renowned theoretical mathematician, was another. Then there was the prodigious New Yorker, J. Robert Oppenheimer, who came to Harvard in the fall of my father's postgraduate year and graduated with a *summa* in chemistry three years later. He went on to direct the atomic bomb project at Los Alamos during World War II. But in 1954 he came under political attack and his security clearance was revoked because of earlier friendships with members of the Communist Party and his opposition to the hydrogen bomb. (Oppenheimer nevertheless was honored nine years later with the Atomic Energy Commission's Enrico Fermi Award for scientific achievement in atomic energy and was director of the Institute of Advanced Studies at Princeton University at the time of his death in 1967.)

Father told me that he found Oppenheimer "a little precious and perhaps a little arrogant but very interesting, full of ideas." Edsall's recollection was kinder: "He was a phenomenal person, with immense intellectual power and intense interests in literature, philosophy and other subjects that went far beyond science." Both were surprised that Oppenheimer turned out to be such an outstanding administrator at Los Alamos. Father and Edsall came to know Oppenheimer better when the three were doing postgraduate work at Cambridge University in England and together took a trip to Corsica that turned into a somewhat mysterious adventure.

···

His brain already buzzing, my father spent a postgraduate year at Harvard taking advanced courses in mathematics, thermodynamics and organic chemistry, subjects that would become vital to his future career. Edsall was still at Harvard, too, as a first-year student at the medical school. In the spring of 1924 the pair left Cambridge, Massachusetts, for Cambridge, England, and the university there that was as noted for science as Oxford was for the arts. Before starting, however, they went to Austria to learn German, spending the summer in Graz under the wing of Otto Loewi, who twelve years later shared the Nobel Prize in Physiology or Medicine for discoveries relating to the chemical transmission of nerve impulses.

By October 1925 Father and Edsall were both busy in Cambridge University's new department of biochemistry, established by Sir Frederick Hopkins and guided by such giants as J.B.S. Haldane and G.S. Adair. Their friends Mirsky and Anson were already there, and Oppenheimer arrived in Cambridge in the fall of 1925 to work in the new field of quantum mechanics at the Cavendish Laboratory. It was some years later that they also met John Kendrew and Max Perutz, who together won the Nobel Prize in Chemistry in 1962 and became lifelong friends of Edsall and my father.

Hopkins's department was a center for research on red blood cells and other heme (blood) proteins, which became Father's pet subject and eventually the focus of his scientific career. But he stayed for only one term, then transferred to University College, London, to work toward his Ph.D. with another Nobelist, Archibald Vivian "A.V." Hill, who was studying the dynamics of muscle as revealed through the muscular contractions of tortoises. This led Hill to a description of oxygen-binding by hemoglobin, the field in which Father later distinguished himself.

Meanwhile, the trip to Corsica with Oppenheimer took place in the spring of 1926. I heard the story many times, both from Father and from Edsall.* Edsall and a boyhood friend, Francis Fergusson, had been worried about Oppenheimer's mental state. He had been working ferociously and seeing a psychiatrist, according to Edsall. Father, an inveterate walker and hiker throughout his life, was also ready for a break. A walking trip would do them all good.

Oppenheimer seemed to be fine at the outset and the three friends were having dinner in a Corsican town prior to moving on to Sardinia when, suddenly, according to Edsall, Oppenheimer said he had to return to England because he had "left a poisoned apple on Blackett's desk." He was referring to Patrick Blackett, an experimental physicist at the Cavendish, whose charm and scientific skill could have made him Oppenheimer's rival. By the next day, Oppenheimer had departed. Father and Edsall, although mystified, traveled on (despite my grandfather Wyman's fear that they'd be killed by Sardinian bandits). When they got back to England, Oppenheimer seemed to be well. So did Blackett. Whatever the truth, Oppenheimer, Edsall and Father remained friends into the 1950s, when Father was called on to defend the Los Alamos chief in an interview with two men from the FBI regarding Oppenheimer's political loyalties.

---

*It is also described in a book of letters and recollections edited by Alice Kimball Smith and Charles Weiner (*Robert Oppenheimer: Letters and Recollections*, Harvard University Press, 1980).

Armed with his Ph.D. from University College, my father returned to Harvard in 1927, initially as an instructor in zoology, then as a teaching assistant and tutor in L.J. Henderson's course in biology. Father also worked with Edwin Cohn, a pioneer in understanding blood proteins and how to separate them—a discovery that proved vital in treating wounded soldiers during World War II. At the time, Cohn, with Edsall and others, was studying the solubility of proteins and their electrical properties. Father was working on the dielectric constants of fluids—studies related to the uptake and discharge of oxygen in large molecules such as the heme protein in red blood—which eventually showed how red blood cells act as a pump to take up oxygen and carry off carbon dioxide.

Father's life wasn't all scientific grind, however. He and Edsall were in England when the great English mathematician and philosopher, Alfred North Whitehead, moved to Harvard in 1924. (Oppenheimer and the visiting Bertrand Russell had attended his seminar in "mathematical suppositions of science" that fall; Oppenheimer received a B grade.) Father and Edsall met Whitehead after their return from England. Edsall recalled that "neither of us ever attended one of his classes," but they did become part of an eclectic group that was invited to drop in on Sunday evenings at the Whiteheads' apartment overlooking the Charles River.

Edsall described these *soirées* in his "Story of Two Interacting Lives," written in 1985. The conversation, he recalled,

> often . . . went on till midnight, sometimes into the small hours, and it ranged over everything—politics, religion, history, philosophy, science, personal recollections; anything might turn up and lead to fresh and unexpected vistas . . . Whitehead's appearance was one of great benignity, which was indeed a reflection of his nature; his sense of humor was keen, but the sharpness and boldness of his mind could lead to sudden vistas of unconventional

thought, expressed in a deceptively gentle tone. Evelyn Whitehead [his wife] too was most exceptional—part Irish, part French and Spanish, she grew up in Brittany and had to master the English language after her marriage. She cared deeply about people, with a great capacity for love and appreciation; but for a few individuals she was also capable of intense dislike. Fortunately both Jeffries and I were among those she valued.

Among other habitués, Edsall recalled, were Philip Johnson, the architect, and Felix Frankfurter, later to become a Supreme Court justice, both then groping toward their eminent careers.

It had been just under a decade since Father had begun the studies at Harvard that transformed his life. The youth with the telescope had grown into a young man with his head in the stars. He had set his sights on the frontiers of science and had been accepted by the Olympians in his field. The worlds of Wellesley and Gloucester had expanded into the universe of ideas. And, like travel in any universe, it would take some surprising turns.

Later Father would take me with him to parts of that world. I remember in 1969 sitting beside him in the very steep amphitheater of London's Royal Society, hearing what Father described as "an amusing if rather inflated lecture, which gave you a chance to see the old London as it survives." And in 1954, when I worked for a publishing company in London, he took me to visit his old mentor, A.V. Hill, at his home outside the city. There I saw the aged tortoises, on which Hill and my father had worked thirty years earlier, plodding around the professor's hilltop garden.

Still earlier, before Whitehead's death in 1947, Father took me to meet the philosopher. I remember that Whitehead had an enormous cranium, which I supposed contained all sorts of fabulous thoughts.

Mrs. Whitehead had false teeth that threatened to fall out during her lively talk. It was her trademark to have the walls of their book-lined sitting room always painted dull black. And over the mantelpiece hung a black glass mirror in which one's reflection appeared like a fish in a dark pool. It seemed a perfect metaphor for the intellectual curiosity they all shared. But the next turn in the road for Father would be marriage and family life.

Chapter 4

Courtship

Father was unfamiliar with women when he met my mother, on a train, the year after he got back from England. And my mother, Anne Cabot, did not much like men, having been bullied by four older brothers.

He was twenty-seven and she was twenty-five. They were on their way to a house party on the shores of Lake Champlain in Vermont. My mother was a cousin of Father's classmate, Will Forbes, which must have set up a social connection. And my scholarly father was the absolute opposite of Mother's gay-blade brothers, which must have appealed to her. At that time he had started his job as an instructor at Harvard. She was taking courses at Radcliffe, tailored to fit her dyslexia, and was living at home in Brookline, working toward a degree in English History. Both solitary, both intellectual, they made a natural pair. But their romance was not destined to run smoothly.

So far, my father's only account to me of their courtship was an amused memory of my charming and whimsical Grandfather Cabot, who saw them kissing on the library sofa and complained to my mother the next day of her "kitchen manners."

But I recently stumbled on two small packets of letters tied up in fine string and addressed in my mother's neat angular hand. Preserved for more than seventy years by my father, these were letters Mother had written to him during their six months' engagement. So far I have not found his letters to her, though they once existed.

It is clear from what she wrote that, in spite of the train ride to Champlain and occasional meetings that winter, Mother and Father barely knew each other. Then, in the middle of June, some kissing and hugging one rainy night in Concord blew my mother away and led to a secret betrothal. One week later Father departed on a solo walking trip in Romania's Carpathian Mountains while Mother stayed at home and wrote daily adoring letters to him care of Barclay's Bank in London. When I showed them to my brother, Jeff was horrified at her passion. He told me if someone had written to him like that, he would have fled. John Edsall, Father's lifelong friend, was amused. "I think your father naively felt Romania would be a nice thing to do, as a sort of farewell to his single life."

My mother's ecstatic letters showed a side of her I never knew and that I now find funny and endearing. "Jeffries, I love you and that is the long and short of it," she wrote to his departing ship. "My one desire is that we should get married as soon as possible so nothing will ever separate us again." This opening salvo of just three paragraphs was written on June 21, the longest day of the year and my father's birthday, though she didn't yet know that about him.

"Perhaps gradually we shall work through our shyness," she continued. "I begin to think it was a miracle that we ever found each other. But now that we have found each other, Oh Jeffries everything lies before us . . . I can't wait for our life to begin, it will be so full and so grand. In the meantime, enjoy your trip but make it short . . ."

Three days later she was in North Haven, Maine, with her sister Susan and her cousin Lucy Fiske. "I begin to think you are as much afraid as I. We must learn at least not to be afraid of each other. I think we succeeded that night on the Sudbury road." The letter breaks off to mention a sail on Penobscot Bay, then concludes with an ardent reminiscence about a drive from New Hampshire's Mount Monadnock, "with the frogs, the watery moon and the delicious night smells. Did you let the rug slip on purpose so I could pull it around you again?"

On June 28 she was counting days and remembering their encounter at a Boston concert. "It is only just two weeks last night since we went to the Pops together and so disgraced ourselves in the eyes (and ears) of my family, and only a scrap more than a week since Concord, but it seems like months, almost years."

Even then, there must have been airmail and the new transatlantic telephone cable, but they didn't use them. Mother had posted thirteen letters and Father had been gone twenty days when his first letters from London reached Mother in Brookline. "My doubts have gone in an instant and I am entirely yours," Mother wrote in reply on July 12. The next day she confided in Susan. The day after that she told her parents and brothers. Her news caused an uproar.

"My Dearest Jeffries," she wrote on the fourteenth. "You must come back immediately if you ever want to see me again. I am in the clutches of my family and entirely overwhelmed . . . My father and mother are more than staggered. I really believe that they think I have lost my head." And, in another letter she wrote, "You must come home anyway because I want you and now I need you."

Her parents, of course, wanted to know why Father had left and when he would return. Mother didn't know. Her letters, all addressed to Barclay's Bank, were forwarded, first to a bank in Budapest, then via Hungary to Romania. It is a miracle that Father ever received them and a delight that he saved the letters so long and so carefully.

Though he quit London about July first, Mother got his last letters from there on July 29. After that there must have been silence.

She spent August in Maine with the family. Her parents' view, that Father "had amazing impertinence" and Mother showed "lack of judgment and common sense" to act so abruptly, began to prevail. On September 4 she wrote a curt note breaking off the engagement.

By September 15, however, my father was back and they had met. "Yes," she wrote him in Gloucester, "marriage is certainly out of the question for us both for the present . . . Until I have found myself, there is no other job for me." But the door was not closed.

As arranged before the engagement, Mother herself was now leaving with Susan for an academic year at Cambridge University in England. "In the meantime," her letter went on, "at least until I sail, I hope we can see a lot of each other and enjoy each other's company."

⋯

This time, Mother was the one abroad and Father the one left at home. But the month of enjoying each other's company had done its job. "There is no longer room for doubt," she wrote him from the S.S. *Scythia*. "We understand each other now in a way we didn't dream of before." Two days later she was reminding Father of "buying the ring" a week earlier and "having that glorious swim" the next day.

Reassured by their September encounters, Mother's letters that fall of 1928 became very flirtatious and cocky. She wrote of meeting "five Englishmen and one wife" at a dance on board ship. She complained that Jeffries was too formal a name, while Jeff reminded her of Mutt and Jeff, and threatened to call her fiancé "You." A view from their future home didn't matter, "as we shall probably never bother to look out the windows." A lonesome letter from him moved her; "but this morning I have hardened my heart and have no more pity for you." He wrote that he couldn't work until they were married; she challenged him to "forget about me for just a little while." And she sauced "Tit for Tat!" about his trip to the Carpathians and her removal to England.

Mother was enjoying herself. She and Susan, who was four years younger and in the throes of a depression, were living as paying guests at Newnham Grange with an American connection of Charles Darwin. "Lady D," as she called Maud Darwin in the letters, was a gregarious and energetic Victorian who reminded my mother of the White Queen in *Alice*. Mother was working on a thesis about English church laws under historian George Macaulay Trevelyan, whom she found to have "very little humor or lightness but great simplicity and charm." There were dinners, concerts and plays, encounters with interesting people. "I am already well settled in and again in pursuit of my clergymen," she wrote Father on October 26. "All I have to do is read endless biographies and correspondences and a little of Hansard's *Parliamentary Reports* and go to Trevelyan whenever I can't think of what next to do."

Their correspondence gave Mother a chance to tell Father about herself. There was a long letter about her family, which she felt "elated" to have "dropped off like lead into the sea." There was her adored Cabot father, "who has always likened himself to David Harum's dog who didn't feel at home without his fleas to bother him," a reference to his six children; her Codman mother, whose family she found "dull, commonplace and usually pig-headed"; and the brothers whose influence "appeared like four great high walls imprisoning me." She compared England to her once-contented "life of the past few years when I have spent every evening at home and hardly seen a soul from one end of the day to the other, not even my family." She described the solitary pleasures of North Haven, the freedom to "do absolutely as one pleases: eat and sleep and read and sail and chop trees."

There were worries about her sister Susan, jokes about her own bad spelling, comments on books and music. Sitting by the fire at night in England, she wrote my father a long silly "dissertation" on the value of old clothes, "all the pleasant experiences they bring back to mind and the sense of freedom and solid comfort they give when worn." And she described the place where she and my father should live when they got married: "with tobacco and pipes on the mantelpiece and books on the floor, comfortable chairs that look well-worn and no silly muslin curtains on the windows or odd knickknacks to collect dust . . . As I turned my head just now," she concluded that Sunday evening of November fourth, "my eye fell on Dürer's etching of St. Jerome in his cell with the lion and the lamb. He had the right kind of room."

By November 10, Mother was determined to abandon England. "I don't get more than one letter a week from you and yet you write me every day," she said. Eleven days later she reflected, "How strange it all is when you think we have only known each other not yet nine months and, for more than seven of those, we have been separated and what's more by oceans . . . I count the days to the time when I can hear from you as to my proposal for returning."

My father, meanwhile, had been visiting the Cabots at their big house in Brookline. "Don't let the family overpower you," she wrote. "I see no reason why you should be always having to go out to see them. They are so insinuating, I am almost afraid of their casting their spell over you." In another letter, she was "amused when Mother said she was beginning to feel quite at home with you. After your letter in which you said she slept all evening, I should say she did."

The plan had been for Mother and my Aunt Susan to stay in England until June. But by November 24, the family seemed to have come around. Their preference about a wedding, she wrote to Father, "was about what I expected: small if desired, but standard church and reception. But what is more to the point, they seem ready to have us marry whenever we want." And two days later, "If we do it at short notice, preparations cannot be as elaborate . . . The only reasons for my staying here are purely Spartan and Puritanical, just to show it can be done."

Jeffries Wyman and his wife, Anne McMaster Cabot, a few years after their marriage. (Photographer unknown; collection of the author.)

By November 28, the sisters had booked passage on the *Berengaria* for December fifth. Mother had told Lady Darwin of their change in plans and wrote Father, "She was grand. She insists you used to play the cello"—something I'm sure he never did; he couldn't carry a tune. She and Susan arrived in New York on December 11 and made their own way by train back to Boston.

Chapter 5

Marriage and Children

My parents' wedding took place that December of 1928 in the First Parish Church of Brookline, a Unitarian stronghold that suited their eclectic views better than Grandma Cabot's Episcopalian church on Hammond Street. After a short honeymoon in New Hampshire, they moved into an apartment in Cambridge. One night some dinner guests encountered them there, fresh from their baths, cheerfully chasing each other around the small parlor with damp towels, while the forgotten dinner burnt on the stove. Things were off to a good start.

By the following fall they had moved out to Brookline and I was born on November 6, 1929, in a small yellow farmhouse on the side of Route 9, which belonged to the Cabots' neighbor, Theodore Lyman. My brother, the fourth Jeffries in line, was delivered in a hospital a year later on November 20. And, not long after that, we moved into the brick house our parents had built next door to Grandma Cabot's, on the top of the hill.

I like to recall the house as it was with my mother there, in the years before she got sick.

Mother and Father at North Haven, Maine, around 1930—notice her feet; she found this to be a comfortable stance. Both are wearing clothes that she made. (Photographer unknown; collection of the author.)

I remember the sound of the doors to the linen closet opening as she stored sheets and towels in the hall opposite my bedroom. I think of looking down on her as she read a book on the lawn below my window, her face tranquil, her short brown hair parted in the middle and brushed back over her ears. I can see her straightforward gaze and wry smile as she asked about a note that I had pinned to her pillow in formal complaint at some perceived injustice the day before.

I loved trailing her into the kitchen in the morning to consult with our cook about meals for the day, and I was there when Mary blew off her eyebrows trying to light the oven one night. I marveled at the ceremony with which Mother mixed salad dressing in a spoon at the table, finally turning it onto the lettuce. I remember the dish of dates and nuts that made an easy dessert at lunch. Here, in my cellar many years later, is the brown paper notebook where she recorded household details in her tidy angular writing. I note with amusement that she thought I was not eating enough at age two or so.

She and my father made rather peculiar parents. I had a passion for nicknames and still have three or four that go with various times in my life. Our parents refused to be called Mummy and Daddy, so I got the idea of calling them "Marmy" and "Farmy" after I read Louisa May Alcott's *Little Women*. Father, surprisingly, liked the idea and retained my name for him always. But Mother objected; Marmy sounded too much like marmalade, or like smarmy, perhaps. To me she was always Mother.

I can feel her presence as she stood us by the sink in our east bathroom, making us swallow cod liver oil before brushing our teeth, then telling us about the 1-4-3 flash from Minot's Light, off Cohasset, saying that it meant "I love you." I remember our shared delight as Jeffy and I watched the putt-putt boat that she'd given us dart around the bathtub, fueled by a votive candle that shone through its tin windows. But I'm still puzzled by a strange memory, in which Mother would strap us to an ironing board and stick us out a window to catch the sun. I can't believe that this nightmare really occurred but, when I asked Father about it, he said, "It's quite possible; she had her own ideas of such things."

As I look back, it seems to me that Mother understood and took my side, without being a dope or a sap. She and Father would half-laughingly tell us to "Do as I say, not as I do," if we protested about some scolding. And if we complained that other children were allowed to wear lipstick or stay up till midnight, the response would be, "just because they do it, doesn't mean you have to do it too," which always made me feel loftier than the poor "they."

One year we had a German nanny, a former judge who had fled her Nazi homeland. Abashed at her new role, the nanny was easy to torment. Jeffy and I drew dirty pictures and showed them to her; she was horrified. When she bathed, she would lock herself into our bathroom. We would draw up a chair, reach for the key on the high lintel and rattle it in the lock. Nanny would leap out of the tub and rush to the door as if defending herself from an army. Mother told us we were being cruel, but she told the nanny she should look for a more suitable job.

Once Jeffy and a friend set fire to an old car that was stored in my grandmother's barn. There was a great to-do about it but I can't remember any terrible consequences. On the other hand, when Jeffy and I threw stones through all thirty-two windows in the large garage that housed Uncle Bob Paine's cars and the squash court, we were made to apologize to that terrifying old Mandarin, who always sat with his back to the light, squinting at us through diamond eyes. And for months we had to contribute to the windows' repair by surrendering our allowances of one penny a week.

Sometimes our parents' pragmatism backfired, though. When my mother and father caught me hiding a smoldering cigarette in my bed one day, they decided I should be taught the dangers of fire.

Together they sat me down in the nursery and held a match to the side of my left hand. I don't remember exactly how it went, but one of them held the match while the other gripped my hand. It lasted only a moment and didn't really hurt, but I insisted on wearing my arm in a sling for a day or two until everyone was shocked and on my side. I cherish the faded scar and I still smoke, so it didn't work— but I look back on their effort with amusement and admiration.

Best of all was Mother's unfailing sense of humor. One April Fool's Day I cut off the toes of all the neatly rolled stockings in her top bureau drawer. Then I watched as she unrolled one pair after another and found every pair of stockings snipped. It was 1941 and there would be no more silk stockings until the end of the war. But after an initial gasp, my mother laughed.

I still have a cigar box of cut-out dolls that we worked on together. Mother helped me to create fanciful costumes with tabs that hooked over the shoulders or around the waists of these paper figures. She taught me to cook, starting with fudge and frosting. She encouraged me to read and to write my own stories, and paid the library back when I cut an inspiring photo of a Vanderbilt mansion out of a book from the Boston Athenaeum. She took me on early-morning bird walks on a nearby estate and allowed me to help transplant the wild hepaticas and lady slippers she and Father had dug up in the town dump. She taught me to ride horses and, over my father's objections, bought me a shaggy black puppy, half setter, half poodle. We named her Duna, after the Forbes family launch at Naushon.

Although Mother and Father disagreed about the dog, it was clear that they were closer to each other than they were to us. Each of them had friends and they often had guests for dinner. But basically they did things together. Father made some wooden book stands that fit onto an armchair so Mother could read and knit at the same time. And he suggested decorations for her sewing projects. I have kept a summer coat that he painted with green and blue leaves and I still have a curtain embroidered with a huge vase of flowers that he designed for her during World War II as a blackout curtain.

Perhaps they were both elusive. They would take us with them on long Sunday walks and Father would make up wonderful stories to suit our interests. But, if we started to lag, they would leave us in the woods, saying they'd be back soon. Once Jeffy and I were abandoned near a small pond in Dover. Time stretched on and suddenly a long black snake slithered out of the water and crossed the path in front of us. We were still trying to reassure each other when our parents returned. Another time, they took us to visit Mother's uncle, Walter Cabot, and his bird-like wife. Our wizened great-uncle was sitting in bed with the shades drawn and a black umbrella over his head; to Aunt Katherine's distress, we were given sandwiches from home and told to stay outdoors while the grownups had lunch.

One summer, they left us with the cook and maid in Brookline while they went on a month-long trip to England and Norway. We would have been about six or seven and, as the weeks stretched on, we wondered if they'd gone forever. But when they left, they solemnly promised to take our present to the Queen of England: a brown paper parcel containing old kitchen spoons and similar treasures. Years later Father confessed they had dumped the package before they left Boston Harbor but they had understood our gesture and were amused.

Another summer our parents planned an expedition to Guatemala with Thomas Barbour, a director of the United Fruit Company. Jeffy and I were sent off to camp. However, I'd just had whooping cough and was still coughing. Our doctor said I was no longer contagious. But when I got to camp I was put into isolation and spent a frightening day or two peering out the window until I saw Mother and Aunt Susan, who had come to rescue me. As he had done during their engagement, Father went off as planned to

Guatemala with his friend. But Mother gave up the trip to save me and instead took me to visit her aunt, Elise Cabot Forbes, on Naushon Island.

···

I loved my mother and we were really close, but I'm haunted by the fact that she never felt as easy with Jeffy. He and I were quite different from the beginning. While I was cocky and independent, my younger brother was shy and cuddly. He used to follow Mother around like a puppy, and I remember one morning she turned on him and told him to "get out from underfoot." We were both hanging around as she worked on some project downstairs but, in this case as in others, he got the blame and I didn't.

Aunt Susan doesn't agree, but I wonder now if this wasn't a holdover from Mother's own youth, with older brothers who could do no wrong in my grandmother's eyes and who had no time for their bookish sister. A childhood photo of Mother in Maine shows her in a pinafore, playing "horsie" alone on the porch with a ferocious scowl on her face.

Susan was young enough to be treated as a pet by the boys, while they saw their older sister, my mother, as a nuisance and oddball. I think she adored her father, who wrote her letters addressed to "Darling Anna Panna." But my grandfather died from a stroke when I was three and, without his support, I am sure Mother always resented the fact that Grandma Cabot had never defended her against her older brothers.

In this connection, it seems very odd that Mother chose to live next door to her mother. The only way I can explain it is that Grandpa was still alive when they moved. Meanwhile, her brothers had married and moved out to Dover. Mother, I think, must have believed that at last Grandma would recognize her. Indeed, we spent almost half of our time in the big house next door. I would go there in the morning and follow Grandma while she restocked the bird feeders or arranged huge bowls of flowers cut from the garden. The door was always open to the big hall with its two Copley portraits, the five-foot bronze stork, the grandfather clock and the grand piano. There were always people around: servants at the back of the house, Grandma receiving in the library, an elderly relative or someone in residence upstairs. A photograph shows the four of us posed with her Irish terrier, Paddy, in the corner of her parlor, where we had tea so often.

The trouble was that I don't believe my grandmother had any idea how angry and wounded my mother felt. So nothing changed. And I was shocked to learn, long after my mother died, that during the times when Mother stayed there after her diagnosis with cancer, she refused to let her own mother come into her sickroom.

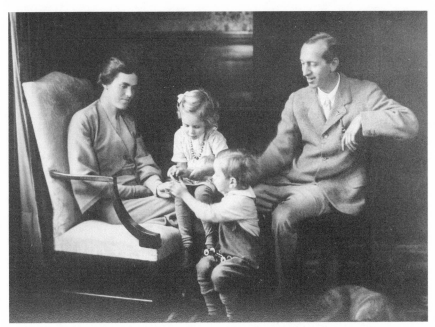

Our family at Grandma's in Chestnut Hill, Massachusetts, around 1934—
Mother, Father, Anne and Jeffy.
(Photographer unknown; collection of the author.)

But that incredibly poisoned relationship seems pale in comparison to Mother's uncomfortable feelings toward her son. Like herself as a child, Jeffy was dyslexic, awkward and needy; perhaps that made his presence painful. In any case, she used to send him to Aunt Susan's in Cambridge one day a week to get him out of the house. And even before Mother fell ill in the summer of 1942, Jeffy, who was then only ten, was sent off to boarding school while I was kept close to home.

Chapter 6

The Starving Armenians

The Starving Armenians, deported by the Turks and left to die in the desert during World War I, were a mythic part of our childhood. We'd be at dinner in Brookline and the maid would come to take our plates and bring the dessert. I might be sitting there, hoping my parents were not paying attention to the fact that I had eaten the hash and corn but left the slimy okra.

Katherine would be neatly moving around the mahogany table, removing the plates one by one, starting with my mother's. The swinging door to the pantry would thump each time. So as she cleared the table there'd be a slight interruption, an interval to review what we had eaten, or not. That was when the Armenians would appear.

My parents might have been engrossed in talk about Winston Churchill or gossiping about one of my mother's brothers. But suddenly Mother would stop and say, "Anne, finish what's on your plate." And my father, from his end of the table, would chime in, "Think of the Starving Armenians. You have all this food and they have nothing."

The Armenians were a grim presence in our household—a specter of helplessness, hopelessness, people in rags, children frightened and crying, hungry and homeless. Was it their fault? What could we do to help? I didn't stop to wonder then just how the food we refused to eat at home in our Boston suburb would get to those distant people. Logic had little bearing here. We were well off and the Puritan ethic dictated that we should think about the needy of the world.

In our Yankee family, however, the ethic was somewhat selective. My parents were genuinely concerned and generous about helping old family retainers, but I suspect both of them thought financial aid was corrupting. People should live the lives they had earned. They were not extravagant and never did things for show. But, while my mother was reasonable about expenses, my father had inherited an eccentric and miserly view of money.

He would protest if we needed new winter coats and complain about the price of butter or the cost of coal for the furnace. "Don't spoil the servants," we would hear him say when it came to giving the cook or the maid a raise or occasional present. Yet we had thick spoony cream from a relative's farm every day for breakfast. And my mother's dressmaking adventures were for fun; the Armenians did not enter into it.

My father insisted that Jeffy and I keep track of our money during the long period when we had an allowance of one penny a week. When the sum reached one dollar, we had to keep written accounts and show him our books. I think he intended this financial regime as a lesson, not an ordeal. At one point, he wrote me a note that read, "I agree with you that the time has come when you can manage your own allowance. But I want you to keep accounts and, what is more important, plan ahead. You must also feel that the allowance is the top figure, just as older people have to do with their incomes."

The Starving Armenians

With inherited wealth, it was significant that he said income, not wages. But our "incomes" were so small and sometimes so unpredictable that I found it hard to take the accounts seriously. Even now, I leave bookkeeping to one horrible session at the end of the year.

My brother was more dutiful than I and his letters from boarding school were full of confusing financial details. In 1946, Jeffy, then fifteen, wrote to Father that "as of March 31" he had ninety-eight cents "on hand," and had received $18.00 from Father, $19.00 in allowance, another $2.00 from Aunt Susan and $2.80 more from Father, for a total of $42.78. Against this, he had spent $39.46, which he itemized—$16.00 for nine car-driving lessons, $4.90 for two Boston dances, fifteen cents on a gardenia for me and sixty cents on a taxi home, including a five-cent tip, and so forth. Sometimes Jeffy was perilously short of cash but Father never panicked. Later that year Jeffy was sent on a summer camping trip to New Mexico. That July he wrote, "I need 7 dollars to get home, plus 45 cents for a raincoat." A note from Father on the back of the postcard suggests he intended to "send $10."

The campaign was also morally based. If we had bought gum or comic books at the little store down the hill on Route 9, we were not just wasting money; the gum would rot our teeth and the comics would rot our brains.

At the same time, Father would say, "If you see something you really want, you should buy it. You may never get the same chance again." Once he bought a marble mantelpiece on its way to the dump from a house in Cambridge and had it installed in place of the nice wooden mantel in our parlor. Most of his clothes were purchased inexpensively at the Harvard "Coop." But he had four fox-colored Harris tweed jackets and two suits tailored for him in London. In 1944, he bought a one-third share in a forty-three-foot sloop (of which more later) along with two of my Cabot uncles.

49

*Young Jeffy at North Haven, 1935.
(Author photo.)*

The sense of guilt and *noblesse oblige* has pursued both me and my brother. A spendthrift myself, I recently refused to take part in a family party when I learned that the bash would cost $250 per person, require the attendance of 400 guests to cover the cost of drinks, dinner and dancing, be arranged by an "events firm" and have no public purpose.

Right away, I thought of the Starving Armenians. I could imagine homeless Bostonians, with their noses pressed to the chain-link fence that would separate them from the party tent on the waterfront. The family would look callous and foolish, I felt. Then it dawned on me that I'd spent four times the admission price of the party to travel first class to Europe, on a coat and on a CD player. What a hypocrite! The real reason I didn't sign up for the party was that big groups made me nervous and I was afraid of being a wallflower.

The issue came up again in a more serious context. Feeling muddled and a little depressed, I'd been seeing a psychiatrist. She was enormously helpful and fun to talk to. But I always felt I was wasting her time on my trivial problems. My wonderful therapist must be itching to deal with really sick people.

I introduced the subject with her one day. "What about the Starving Armenians?" I asked.

"If you really care about the Armenians, why don't you send them some money?" she said.

The whole thing is fraught with ambivalence. Each year, I spend hours drawing up a list of charities to which I send contributions. The total does not exceed five percent of my income. But deciding which agencies or schools should get $50 and which $500 makes me feel like God.

It also makes me feel like a sucker. I donate to political campaigns that are going nowhere and respond to emergency calls from Democrats to whom I've already contributed. And when the police and firemen call up, I always put a small check in the mail. Are these the Starving Armenians? Will they let me be murdered in my bed or see my house burn down if I refuse their pleas?

I wonder what Father would think of all this. By the time he died in 1995, he had lived and worked in Europe for forty years, carefully maintaining his tourist visa in order to avoid paying Italian or French taxes. When he visited America, he always dashed in to see his financial advisor and gloated about any increased holdings. All the same, he belonged to two clubs in Boston and, on his rare visits to them, enjoyed their sumptuous dinners. And, when I was trying to paint, he would say, "Don't worry if it isn't right. Try again. Paper is cheap."

In his old age, Father loosened the purse strings and arranged gifts to Jeffy and me and to his stepson Dimitri. It helped that these gifts were a hedge against death duties. But he also made gifts to the young men who had taken care of his household in Paris, though not, that I can remember, to charities. Certainly nothing went to the Starving Armenians.

Money, whether earned or inherited, was in my father's view a means to pursuing the kind of life you preferred. It allowed you to take the interesting job, not the most lucrative. You could stand up to the boss or the system and risk being fired. You could own a share in a sailboat, pay the upkeep on a house in the country, buy a mantelpiece or a beautiful African statue. Still, the outlay should be prudential. When I bought a house of my own in 1968, Father approved; he considered the house a good investment and later remarked on the property's rising value. But if I bought a dress or took friends out to dinner, he would ask how much it cost and, raising his eyebrows in shock, would say, "What?" or "As much as all that?"

Father passed his financial values on. My brother lives in old shirts and sneakers, eats in diners and stays in simple motels on his Florida fishing trips. But Jeff has the best Hardy reels, has stalked salmon in Siberia and, most amazing to me, has established a trust to preserve open land at the Cabot family place in Maine and a post-doctoral fellowship in my father's name at Harvard. It's as though he sees money as filthy lucre and wants to get rid of it.

In some ways I deplored Father's meanness with money. He was still giving ten-cent tips in the 1970s. Once he came with us to Maine carrying a $100 bill, which was too much to break for a bundle of groceries; Jeff and I paid and he got through two weeks with the $100 intact. His wives were constantly starved for cash. But in his eccentric way, Father taught us the value of money and made us feel the Armenians were always there if we squandered it.

Chapter 7

Death and Dislocation

It's funny the tricks memory plays. I can see my tall, big-boned mother and can recall her warm, wooleny smell but I cannot remember the sound of her voice. It's as though one day she was there and the next day she was gone. In fact, she was sick for fifteen months before she died of Hodgkin's lymphoma in September 1943. I was thirteen and she was just forty. Today she would likely have been cured.

We were in North Haven, Maine, when her illness first showed its face. Father had brought Jeff and an English boy named Michael Hankey to the island. I'd gone ahead with Mother, who seemed to be coming down with the flu. We were staying in the big shingled "cottage," started as a camp by my great-grandfather, Walter Channing Cabot, in 1893. Because there was no stove in the main house, we were cooking and eating in a smaller building named "Billy's Kitchen" where, in high summer, all the children ate at the far end of the point overlooking the Billy Cove (named after the devil because the cove had a sprawling ledge, covered at high tide).

The main house, or "Big House" as we called it, was like a maze, with a central hall full of slickers and tennis rackets and a staircase up to a guest room and two tiny bedrooms, named "the Slits," over the big open parlor. Another staircase led to Grandma's room. Outside, stairs scaled two sides of the house, and the three bathrooms had skylights. When all of my cousins were there, we used to play a form of hide-and-seek called "Beckon," using the rims of the tubs to hoist ourselves through the skylights onto the roofs and down those outside stairs.

But that June of 1942 we Wymans were alone on the point. Mother and Father were sharing the guest room while Jeff and I slept nearby in the Slits. I knew something was wrong when Mother, who had been staying in bed feeling ill, suddenly leapt up and chased me out of her room with a broom. I'd been annoying her by throwing a ball out the window, but her reaction was scary. It was so different from Mother lying in the hammock with her book and her pipe, ready to talk or read aloud, so unlike her walking along the Creek Path, gathering balsam and mosses so we could make a pillow or tray-garden. Suddenly I was sure Mother would hit me with the broom if she could catch up, and I ran away from her as fast as I could.

Perhaps I was still worried when, a few mornings later, I was alone with Mother at the Big House and heard her call out for help. She had come down the outside stairs by the Slits, which landed on a rocky outcrop, and was stuck. I found her standing on the rough gray stone, her face toward the house, gripping the stair rail. She asked me to help her and told me to hold on so that she wouldn't fall. Following her instructions, I stood behind her, putting my skinny arms around her ribs. But she said it hurt or didn't feel safe. So I tried to shift my grip and all of a sudden she toppled, rigid and white, into the crack between the rocks and the house. Her eyes were half closed. Her body was totally stiff. I thought she was dead.

I must have screamed for Father, who was making breakfast in Billy's Kitchen, 500 yards away through the spruce woods. Now I can't hear my own voice either. But I remember Father running, running along the dirt path, bending over my mother, calling her name. "Anne! Anne, can you hear me? Anne!"

Somehow we carried Mother into the house and onto the sofa, where she revived. The island doctor came and told us he thought she might have undulant fever from unpasteurized milk. She should go back to Boston as soon as possible, he said.

The doctor must have made the arrangements but I don't remember what they were, or how we got off the island. I know that Mother went in an ambulance from Rockland to Brunswick, where she was put on a train. Were we with her or did we follow her in the car? I think now that she must have gone straight to the Massachusetts General Hospital, but where did we go? When I asked her fifty years later, Aunt Susan could not remember either.

All through the summer of 1942 I had no idea what was wrong with my mother and no one would tell me. I found out for myself that fall when I knew something was going on and steamed open a letter from Aunt Nell Cabot to Father. I saw that she was consoling him because Mother had cancer and would probably die. I'm not sure what Mother had been told but I realized then that Father, Grandma, Aunt Susan and even the Paines on the other side of our hill must have known. Yet no one would talk about it to me. And I didn't dare ask.

There were times when Mother seemed better. But it didn't last. I remember being with her when she had her second seizure. It was a gray autumn day and we set out to walk together to the open fields of The Country Club in Brookline. We hiked down Grandma's field, crossed Heath Street and got as far as the club's stone boundary wall when Mother said she was feeling wobbly. I remember we sat with our backs to the stones. Four months into her illness then, Mother refused to believe her condition was fatal and I didn't mention it. But there was a shadow over our conversation as we discussed my future of going to dances, meeting boys and learning to get on in the world. I still can't hear her voice but I recall that Mother was sympathetic, funny and measured as we faced these dire challenges. And I felt very close to her as we headed back up the hill toward home.

The spasms came as we got near our house and she collapsed on our gravel driveway within sight of the front door. It wasn't as bad as the time at North Haven, and I waited beside her until she came to and was able to get indoors and eventually upstairs, onto the chaise in the second-floor sitting room where she spent so much of her time in the long year ahead.

That winter Father went every day to his lab at Harvard; Jeffy was a boarding student at the Eaglebrook School in western Massachusetts and I was at the Winsor School in Boston. Some of the time Mother and I were at Grandma's. Some weeks I stayed nearby with the Paines. In the summer of 1943 Jeffy and I were sent to North Haven with Uncle Harry Cabot and his wife, Aunt O, where, one day, I was confined to my room for some act of defiance. Everything was out of whack and I wanted to be back in our own house in Brookline where there was a chance that things would return to normal and at least we would all be together.

When I did get home, I remember Mother lying by the windows in her upstairs room getting thinner and thinner as the days went by. She looked as if she would break if you touched her and, in the end, she couldn't eat or drink.

I recall that Jeff was still away the morning Father came into my room, his face soaked with tears, to say that Mother had died in the night. I wonder now if he had slept beside her in their double bed. Did he have a chance to talk to her before she died? Did he rush around trying to do something? Did he hold her in his arms as she stopped breathing? I don't know and I don't remember his telling me or my ever asking. Tragedy was something we didn't talk about. Perhaps it's no wonder I can't hear my mother's voice.

There was no time to grieve. It was the opening day of school and I went as though nothing had changed. I didn't know how I was supposed to act so I told some of my classmates to see what they would say. And I think that I was sent home early. I don't remember Jeffy coming home, or where we stayed. I don't even remember Mother's funeral. It must have been at Bigelow Chapel (adjoining the crematory) at Mount Auburn Cemetery in Cambridge because she was cremated. I know that because Mother's ashes, in their plain brown box, are still somewhere in my house. Father planned that we would scatter them over Penobscot Bay or in the North Haven graveyard, but somehow it never happened. Now I would like to bury her ashes in the Wyman family plot at Mount Auburn, along with a memorial to my father. I hate it that their fourteen years of marriage, our years of family life, should remain unmarked.

I wish I could hear Mother's voice and the sound of her laugh. I know she was reserved and I think she was angry about her own childhood. I would like to ask her about all that. I wonder whether she would be proud or indifferent about my own life. I miss her and wonder if she misses me.

The months after Mother's death whizzed by in a blur. John Edsall has told me that Father's Harvard friends worried about him and urged John to get him away from Brookline. They went off on a ten-day walking trip in the Smoky Mountains of North Carolina. Recently Claude Debru, who knew my Father in Paris in the 1980s, wrote me that my father once told him that, during those weeks after Mother's death, Father felt he was going to die.

Jeff and I were assigned to live with Uncle Harry and Aunt O in Dover because they were wealthy and had only one son. At some point in the fall Aunt Susan took me to look at boarding schools. The Baldwin School in Bryn Mawr, Pennsylvania, struck my fancy because it had stone towers and a nice headmistress from New England. Rosamond Cross enrolled me on the spot. Father, alone in Brookline, sought comfort by going to Grandma's every morning for breakfast and often for dinner. But he was miserable. Something had to change and, by February 1944, he had taken a leave of absence from Harvard and signed up with the Navy to work on sonar and smoke screens for the war.

The third terrible blow came within months of Mother's death and Father's disappearance. I was away at school the following spring when I heard from Aunt Susan in Cambridge that Grandma Cabot had cancer of the throat and was very ill. Jeffy sent a letter to Father on March 27, 1944, during a school vacation.

"I am with Cousin Ellen [Paine] now and am having great fun," he wrote. "I am about to go to the dentist. Grandma has been very poorly and is very sick. She is only able to suck ice. She cannot talk without having a terrible coughing fit. She never comes downstairs. I come to see her every morning but lately she has been too poorly to see me." Jeffy was keeping up a bold front but Aunt Susan remembered him forlornly walking around and around outside the house where Grandma lay dying.

Nine days later Jeffy wrote again from Dover. The letter, postmarked April 5, on Uncle Harry's stationery, said,

Dear Father, It is too bad you couldn't get off for Grandma's funeral because it was very nice and simple, just the way she would have wished. Everybody came to lunch at Grandma's, I mean the grandchildren and children and the [in-law] aunts and Uncle Charlie [Walcott]. We had a good dinner and then went down to the church where Mr. Trowbridge held a very nice simple service. I didn't see, but Mr. Trowbridge said the church was full of men.

After that we went to [the cemetery in] Forest Hills where he pronounced the benediction. From here we went to a nice tea at Grandma's.

It is awful to think the Big House [in Brookline] has to go and the land will be made into streets and alleys and noisy apartments but I suppose it can't be helped . . . I keep thinking of the walk in the Noannet Valley after the funeral for Mother . . .

Both letters were addressed to Father at the Woods Hole Oceanographic Institution but were forwarded to the Amphibious Training Center in Fort Pierce, Florida. Within eight months Mother and Grandma had gone and, at that point, Jeff and I did not know precisely where Father was.

◆◆◆

Recently, on an errand to Brookline with a boarding-school friend, I drove to Heath Street to see the old family home. The hill is now covered with mini-McMansions, including Grandma's house (now a sprawling brick castle). Our old driveway has been torn up. But a nice watchman, parked beside a sign saying "60 Singletree Road" (it used to be "215 Heath Street"), allowed us to walk in. The house, the gardens and the old oak tree with its long arm had vanished completely. I could guess where the circle by our front door used to be, but the rest was a mysterious hole, overgrown with a chaos of weeds and trees. The only remnant of bygone times was the stone seat at the foot of what is now a skeleton oak tree. The old path to the tennis court is no more and the town reservoir, itself, seems shaggy and its steel-wire fence encroaching.

We did not stay long. But on our return I told my schoolmate about the time Mother drove me to Aunt Susan's in Cambridge. The top of her Model-A roadster was down and I sat beside her, wearing a Carabinieri full-dress helmet of shiny silver with a black ruff of horsehair down the middle. It was a loan from Cousin Ellen Paine and I was proud to show it off to the passing traffic. I must have been about eight at that happy time.

Chapter 8

War Years

Within five months of Mother's death, we three survivors were all on the road.

Father, we thought from his letters, was somewhere at sea doing secret research for the Navy—something glamorous and important, I imagined. Jeff, who had just turned thirteen, was back in exile at the Eaglebrook School in Deerfield. And sometime that fall of 1943 I became a boarder at the Baldwin School in Bryn Mawr. By the end of the following year, our Brookline house had been rented. Soon Grandma's house was sold, torn down and rebuilt by strangers. Like castaways, we would be essentially separated for the rest of our lives, though we didn't yet know that.

Having arranged for Jeff and me to spend our school vacations with Uncle Harry and Aunt O in Dover, Father waved his Kipling's-Cat tail and walked off on his wild lone, keeping in touch with us through letters and occasional visits.

World War II had by then turned in the Allies' favor but there was still work to be done. From March 1944 to July 1946 Father was based at the Woods Hole Oceanographic Institution on Cape Cod, making forays along the Eastern seaboard and into the Pacific in connection with U.S. Navy projects on smoke screens and underwater sound detection, or sonar. When he was around, which was rarely, he lived in a vast stone mansion on Naushon Island, owned since 1843 by the Forbes family. It was a fifteen-minute ride by launch from the laboratory, though he usually chose to cross the rough waters of Woods Hole by kayak.

For my father, it was the beginning of a new life and a new adventure. Five days into his Navy job, Father was organizing a small team of experts in sound, waves and wind. The group included a man named Al Woodcock, "who is much interested in the soaring of birds and has powers of observation amounting almost to genius," he wrote to me in Pennsylvania. "A theoretical man is coming down on Monday and we shall make quite a group, which I hope will grow and prosper. I like them all and I hope we can build a team spirit . . ."

Father was away most of that first year. I saved all of his letters from that time and can reconstruct some of his travels now. So I see that, by March 14, 1944, he was en route to Florida, having stopped off in Washington to spend the day with people in the Bureau of Ships. In May our new guardian, Uncle Harry, wrote me saying, "Your pa's address is the Pacific Ocean and, so far as I know, he could leave nothing more specific." On May 22 Jeffy wrote from school asking, "Have you heard anything from Father? I haven't . . . I don't have any news from home."

That summer Father spent several days in New York, where he met with some people in the Empire State Building and watched a thunderstorm from the fiftieth floor. "The sheets of rain came sweeping by and we watched the flashes [of lightning] strike at first one skyscraper, then another," he wrote.

A pictureless postcard from the Cosmos Club in Washington, postmarked October 10, 1944, disclosed that he was off to Cuba. "I shall be in Miami tomorrow night and in Guantanamo the night after & so on." He had spent Sunday in New York seeing "some wonderful pictures at the Metropolitan [Museum of Art]."

Left to right: Alexander Forbes, unknown person and Jeffries Wyman in Cuba, 1944.
They were flying these planes to make smoke screens.
(Photographer unknown; collection of the author.)

By November, Will Forbes's uncle, Alexander Forbes, a pilot and cartographer, had joined the team in Cuba. A young engineer named David Barnes was coming. Father was sharing a room with Woodcock. The figure for the mean temperature was cut out of his letter, presumably by a censor. But Father was allowed to send a postcard showing Havana's Moro Castle. And his letters—one on "V-Mail" with three dots and a dash signaling V for Victory, posted "c/o Commander, Caribbean Sea Frontier, Fleet Post Office, New York"— described aspects of his work. "One night," he wrote, "I sat up till

2 A.M. writing some very complicated operational plans which we have been using ever since. It is very exciting to see a number of units, some in the air, some on the sea, all maneuvering together to be in the right place at the right time and do what is expected of them.

"Dave," he continued, "was out at sea all day yesterday on a vessel called a YMS. I stayed on shore. Today I am going up in a blimp, so you may think of me as nosing along like a big fish sticking his nose here and there and taking a nibble when he sees something worthwhile. But our nibbles are different from a fish's." He was hoping to go horseback riding in the hills above Guantanamo Bay.

⋯

Clearly Father was having fun. A letter challenging me to write to him more often suggests that I was angry and unforgiving about his absence. But, like him, I was also ready to move on. My boarding school was full of war refugees and the train between Boston and Philadelphia was full of soldiers and sailors. The general hubbub made sense in the wake of the Allied landing at Anzio on January 23, 1944, and the end of the siege of Leningrad about the same time. Father had joined the war effort; I wanted to be part of it too.

On the eight-hour train trip back to school in September 1945, I made friends with a young sailor. A brash fifteen, I persuaded him to take me to the movies in Philadelphia before he put me and my tennis racket on the Paoli Local at Philadelphia's 30th Street station. The interlude was harmless; perhaps we held hands in the dark. But I arrived at the Baldwin School hours late and found a message that the headmistress wanted to see me.

Miss Rosamond Cross, square-chinned and blue-eyed, with short curly blond hair, was funny and sensible like my mother. She interviewed me in her apartment behind the school auditorium. My

Aunt O, said Miss Cross, had called to see if I had reached school safely. What had kept me? she asked. Rising to the occasion and remembering Father's letters, I told her I had met a friend of Father's named Al Woodcock and had gone with him for coffee. When this word reached Father through Aunt O, he noted wryly that Woodcock had been with him in Woods Hole that day. Miss Cross, too, seemed unalarmed. However, I was forbidden to leave the school grounds till Thanksgiving. But, through this lark, I learned that my father was, in fact, momentarily in Massachusetts.

My correspondence with Father continued, sometimes coy and disjointed. My new physics teacher had posed the idea of terminal velocity. I decided to test this on Father. "If a body weighing 125 pounds fell from a 200-foot building, how fast would it be going when it hit the ground? How fast would the body be going if it fell from a plane at 2,000 feet? What if the body was moving forward?"

Father sent a delayed reply from Naushon, enclosing a page of inscrutable calculations and adding a reference to an earlier foray I'd made onto a porch roof at Baldwin. "I did not really think you were serious about the problems, or I would have answered them the first time you asked," he wrote. "You are not thinking of testing my solutions by jumping out of the windows are you? If you had slipped that night you were out on the roof, you might have had a chance to verify them." I hadn't told him, of course, that I'd gone onto the roof to smoke.

Occasionally, Father would appear at school on his way to or from southern ports. I was overwhelmed with pride at the way he got on with Miss Cross and managed to charm all my friends. Uncle Harry and Aunt O also seemed to adore him. And he fitted perfectly into the almost Shakespearean world of the Forbeses at Naushon. But, even though Jeffy and I were well cared for, I felt left out. I wanted to be the apple of Father's eye but I couldn't seem to catch his eye, no matter how hard I tried.

His exploits were unmatchable. One night in the dead of winter he broke his paddle while kayaking back from work through the treacherous currents of Woods Hole. He managed to land on a far part of Naushon and walked home in the freezing dark. His only comment was that he loved the isolation of the island, "when I can let my mind and body follow their own whims."

My own attempts at adventure generally fizzled. During a summer sail along the coast of Maine with Aunt O and Uncle Harry, Aunt O wrote to Father, "We had to send Anne ashore to buy some newspapers because she was so restless and so full of big talk about preferring to sail in the rain." Once when I tried to discuss a recent book by British socialist Harold Laski, Uncle Harry, who was chief trustee of the Boston Symphony and a founder of the World Federalists, told me crossly to stop being such a serious-minded bluestocking.

I missed my mother, who could knit and read at the same time, who smoked a pipe and whose clothes smelled like warm peat. I missed my father, who wrote adult letters about his adventures and his work. And I felt uneasy with the Harry Cabots, who seemed to find me so awkward. There was no one in Dover to do things with and I worried that their son Harry was making a slave out of Jeffy, getting my kid brother to siphon war-rationed gas from one car to another so they could drive off to parties where everyone drank. So I used to take the commuter train into Boston and wander around the book and record shops, winding up at Schrafft's for a chocolate sundae and long heart-to-heart talks with the waitress, Gussie Guiardini.

Early in 1945 Father was in Panama, then in Puerto Rico. After that he and the Oceanographic team continued to sort out their findings in Woods Hole and Father was back at Naushon. The family trustees had offered to let him stay in the ornate Victorian pile called the Stone House in exchange for the tiny rent of $150 a month. A letter from Will Forbes urged him not to worry about the rent. "We had considered your presence on the island and particularly at the Stone House was a stabilizing factor and should be encouraged even if we had to pay you not to leave."

The Stone House had one furnace that warmed the kitchen wing; the family rooms, designed for summertime, had no such comforts. My forty-four-year-old father was in his element. "This is a dream come true," he wrote. "I should like these moments to be prolonged into an eternity. It is not lonely or boring at all, but heavenly, and all the nice things of life seem to be hovering in my mind as I sit here."

Fred and Lucille Schaffner, who worked for the Forbeses, lived in the back of the house to care for him, and he was teaching Lucille to cook. "I give her various hints and suggestions which she takes well," he wrote that October. "She had never eaten an eggplant until the other day." In November Lucille produced baked eels for Father and Will's brother, David, who had come for the weekend. While out on the island, they found a young doe who had caught her leg in a stone wall and died. "Fred and I drove up [in a horse-drawn wagon] this afternoon and brought her back. As a result, we now have about 30 pounds of good venison hanging." He planned to eat the liver for breakfast. Another night, he boasted, "I had a lobster supper all by myself."

Most of the time Father was alone in the huge drafty house. But the island was not uninhabited. "There are five woodcutters living in shanties by Mary's Lake," he wrote that spring. "It was quite romantic to see their lights and smell the smoke of their fires as I rode back from Tarpaulin Cove."

Members of the family came and went, even in the off-season. Will's sister was planning to turn the Stone House into a sort of hotel that summer. Alexander Forbes, who had been with Father in the Caribbean, spent a few nights to discuss their work for the Navy. Once in the late fall Father gave a square dance for twenty people in the big wood-paneled hall of the Stone House. "They are coming over at 8 or 8:30," he wrote, "and I will give them supper at 10:30. I have scalloped quahogs, 2 venison pies, cold venison, hot rolls, tea and coffee, punch, gingerbread and cream planned for them." He would have picked the quahogs himself, and I suppose the abundance of venison resolved the fate of the deer he found in the wall.

Jeffy and I spent part of our Christmas vacation with him at the Stone House, taking long walks down the island to clear the sandy paths of trees felled by a hurricane. Once when Father and I were chopping double on either side of a big log, the head of my axe flew off and sailed between his legs. I was horrified; the axe head could have killed him. But I recall that we kept on working, though on separate logs. And, as we walked home through the beech woods, Father would have told us stories, which he could produce on demand, given a setting or a character. Many of them involved children living near Tarpaulin Cove during the American Revolution when British troops were marauding in Vineyard Sound. "Is that real, Father?" we would ask. But he would never say.

We knew Naushon well. I was seven when Mother first took me there to stay with Grandfather Cabot's sister, Elise. And I had fallen under the spell of its sixteen square miles of beech woods and moors; the sailboats and horses; the idea that, once you passed through the farm gate near Mary's Lake, the only houses ahead were the old farm at Tarpaulin Cove and the little brown cottage on Robinson's Hole at the west end of the island.

While the boys fished or sailed, Holly Forbes and I raced our ponies down the half-mile beach at the Cove or, like Foreign Legionnaires, skidded the ponies headlong down the sand cliffs of the Happy Valley. We slept out at night and scared ourselves with phosphorescence when we jumped naked into the harbor. Once Holly, with her four younger brothers and sisters and Jeffy and me, all painted each other with the bright blue that was supposed to go on a buggy. When Jeffy and I rowed back to the house we were renting that summer, Mother and Father got out a dishpan, stood each of us in it and scrubbed us down with kerosene.

But these years, right after the war, were different. Mother was dead and Father had somehow vanished. Recently my cousin Powell Cabot surprised me by saying, "Your father left on his own affairs and thought he could bring you and Jeffy up by writing letters." Father himself used to say we should have been glad that he wasn't there to boss and harass us like most other parents. Jeffy has told me that he found Father "the perfect parent. He taught me everything I care about." As for me, I am sure that Father was right. He would have been frustrated, strict and erratic if he had stayed and tried to raise us himself. But, by his absence, he made us anxious, perhaps too much so, to live up to his romantic image.

Chapter 9

Sailing Lessons

The Cabot family stronghold in Maine was completely different from the Forbes family's calypso island in Buzzards Bay. Indeed, my great-grandfather left Cape Cod for the island in Penobscot Bay because, he maintained, in Cotuit everyone was asleep half the time. Where Naushon was soothing, North Haven was brisk. Naushon was relaxed and comfortable; North Haven was rustic and competitive.

Everybody on the island sailed. My mother's four older brothers raced dinghies and Herreshoff twelve-footers two or three times a week. The bare pine studs of the Big House parlor and those in the separate dining room where the adults ate were hung with faded triangles of blue and red, pennants that marked their prizes. Father wanted us to be equally able. More than that, however, he wanted us to share his own sense of adventure at being cut off from dry land.

His lessons began in a tricky little sailboat designed for the strong winds of Penobscot Bay and for madcap races through the rocks and currents of its coves and harbors. "If you can sail the North Haven dinghy, you can sail anything," he would say, as we whizzed around the salt creek below the Cabot enclave on Pulpit Harbor.

The wood-hulled dinghy, not much bigger than a skiff, would rock as we boarded it and bob around while we hoisted its single gaff-rigged sail. Father would lower the centerboard, cast off the mooring, back the sail into the wind so we'd fall away from the buoy, and we'd be off.

He was an expert sailor, taught during his boyhood summers in Gloucester by fishermen who had spent years on the Grand Banks. With him on board things went smoothly. But one afternoon, when I was about ten, I went out alone with my dog while the grown-ups napped after lunch. I got neatly away from the mooring and headed downwind with the sail out wide. But when I rounded up too fast, the dinghy swamped. Shaggy black Duna, alarmed by the seawater pouring over the side, jumped onto the seat and got under the tiller. I pushed the dog overboard and watched her swim safely to shore. Then I bailed out the water, which was up to my knees, and sloshed back to the mooring, proud that the boat hadn't sunk.

"You must learn to trust the feel of the boat," Father said as he came out with me to practice downwind turns. I was never quite reassured but I persevered. I wanted to own this skill for myself. Father was scornful of sissies and landlubbers. And he enjoyed taking risks. Later, to follow his dashing example, I learned to fly small planes and, settling on a career as a journalist, I traveled the world writing stories for the *Boston Globe*. Quite often I was spooked by my own adventures.

Then I would think of his voice, urging us on or rising in urgent warning.

When Jeffy and I became teenagers, Father bought a share in *Kestrel*, a sloop owned by two of my Cabot uncles, and took us cruising along the Maine coast. *Kestrel* was one of fourteen Fisher's Island 31 sloops designed and built in the early 1930s by Sidney Herreshoff in Bristol, Rhode Island. She was forty-three feet overall, thirty-one feet on the waterline, with a draft of just over six feet. Considered a "Herreshoff classic," she was designed for racing in Narragansett Bay. Her interior was modified for cruising by Francis Kinney, a designer for Sparkman & Stephens, and installed by the Concordia Yard with five berths, a galley and an enclosed toilet. I know of only three survivors. One was recently being offered by the Kingman Yacht Center in Cataumet, Massachusetts. Another was on offer by Cannell, Payne & Page of Camden, Maine, for an asking price of $98,000.

We never knew this legacy at the time, of course. Sailing was something we could do together, a chance to pit our strength and wisdom against the wild elements, and an occasion to talk and explore. From the time Jeffy was about fifteen and I a year older, we set sail with Father for a week or so in June and perhaps again in September.

Often Will Forbes, our mother's first cousin, came with us. I remember Father's younger wartime friend Henry Stommel was once there. And Jeffy and I brought friends, too. The boat slept five, four in the main cabin and one forward in the pipe-berth, where I loved to lie snug in warm blankets looking through the open hatch at the stars rocking above. It was a cozy house party. Once, while moored off Petit Manan, we discovered that four of us were using the same toothbrush.

Recently I was on Mt. Desert Island on Columbus Day and drove up the tar road to Beech Hill. Almost fifty years earlier Father, Jeffy and I had walked there when it was just a dirt lane. It was there on that bygone afternoon that I learned not to quit. All day, as we drifted up the long fjord called Somes Sound, we teenagers had been losing things overboard: a chart, the deck mop and finally the bilge pump, pushed through an unguarded porthole. Father was disgusted and we went ashore at Somesville to stretch our legs. But when we got back from Beech Hill and had bought a few groceries, he suggested hoisting the sails again. A night wind came up and the moon was full as we sailed past Cadillac Mountain to Southwest Harbor and dropped anchor in the dark. Father, who liked to write poems himself, recited Yeats's "White Birds" as we sat beneath a "blue star of twilight, hung low on the rim of the sky . . ." And we hung out the red and green riding lights before going to sleep.

Confronting known dangers was part of the fun. I remember our sailing over the ledge at the back of Sorrento Harbor. Our sloop had a six-foot keel but the tide was high and the following wind gave us a straight crossing through the hairline passage marked on the chart for shallower lobster boats. His taking the shortcut saved us two hours of sailing and taught us to calculate chances before we took them.

My mother's family used to joke that Father was "the absent-minded professor." But he was as much at home at sea as he was in his Harvard lab. When we decided to stop for supplies in a crowded passage off Jonesport, Father sailed our sloop through the thicket of moored boats and shot up to the massive town dock as though we were in a nimble dinghy. What a mess it would have made if we had been going too fast or too slowly!

The Gloucester fishermen of his youth had taught him every old trick of their trade and that helped when the hazards were unexpected. One sunny midday we ran hard aground on a gravel bank in the Mussel Ridge Channel near Rockland, an hour after high tide. Father was below, writing up the ship's log, while Jeffy or I was steering. He popped out like a cork, his voice raised in dismay. "What have you done?" he cried. But almost at once he was planning a rescue. It would be almost twelve hours before the tide was high again. Meanwhile, as the water ebbed away, the boat would tip on the bare gravel with the danger of filling with water if she fell the wrong way.

Within minutes Father spotted some long spars on the far beach and, in an hour or two, he had showed us how to build a cradle under the sloop, with a line from the top of the mast to the shore and the heavy boom tied out on the opposite side for balance. Then, with the ship secure, he rowed off in the tender and painted a water-color of the rig. As the tide dropped we all went ashore to pick mussels and clams. And when the tide rose again we knocked down the poles and pulled ourselves off with an anchor set out to stern—a process called "kedging," he told us.

Another time, I remember heading for Carver's Harbor in thick fog, noting each buoy and the time it took to sail from one to the next. Suddenly we heard waves breaking on rocks dead ahead. Father slowed the boat by letting out sail and my brother went off in the rowboat to lead us between the shore and an island in the mouth of the harbor. I stood as lookout but couldn't see Jeff in the murk and his voice seemed to come from everywhere. I was scared. Perhaps we could have turned on the engine, but it seldom worked and Father refused to use it. He knew how to creep through the fog under a shaking sail and, when we made it safely, we all felt triumphant. He might have made baked beans on North Haven and brought them along. If so, I'm sure we ate them for comfort that night.

I thought of all this many years later when I was out in the bay, alone in the family's old Crowninshield knockabout, one of only four boats of its kind, built in 1915 and the only survivor still sailing. Seventeen feet on the waterline and just over twenty-eight feet overall, she was a racehorse. The weather was perfect and the wind had done its usual thing of dying at noon, then blowing hard in the afternoon. But when I turned back from my downwind sail, the knockabout not only began lurching like a drunken dancing partner but was leaking. I tried to remember what Father would do and headed from island to island with the sail half-flapping as we had done in Carver's Harbor. That slowed the boat and lessened the strain on the old craft. Then, each time I came to a lee behind some grassy atoll, I let the sail go and stopped to bail. It took ages to limp upwind, but eventually both the boat and I got home safely.

The lurching and leaking, I learned, were caused by a loose keel. But, when our veteran day-sailor had been rebuilt and I elected to sail her around from the boatyard, the knockabout was still fragile and she still leaked—this time from new boards in her sides. I had fourteen-year-old Bear Hopkins, the son of an islander, with me that afternoon. We had just made it out of a calm and around the end of the island when we were caught by the afternoon blow and chased down the bay by a howling tailwind. I remembered how I had filled the dinghy with seawater from that downwind turn when I was ten. I also didn't want the big peaked sail to slam over the boat in a jibe. So I cautiously turned into the wind along the shore in a series of long figure eights, with Bear bailing and grumbling all the way. Father would have been proud of me, although he wouldn't have been so proud when I exhaustedly let down the sail in the harbor and broke the wooden jaws that held the gaff around the mast. Bear, of course, was delighted.

◄►

Father's edicts weren't always successful. As kids, we were told that a bath should be only as deep as his forefinger and he would pull the plug if the tub was fuller than that. But I continued to like a real soak. Once in Milton, when I must have been in my twenties, I had drawn a deep bath. Then Father appeared and attempted to claim it, insisting that I would be in the tub for hours while he could just step in and out. I protested and grabbed his arm; together we managed to pull the loaded towel rack into the water before he backed off.

It was in North Haven, though, that my best revenge came, at the end of a long day. Father, Jeff and I had taken the old rowboat, called *Glitter*, down to the end of the island, two of us rowing and one sitting in the stern. On the way home, with Father rowing behind me, I complained that he was not following my stroke and was bumping my back. "Let Jeffy row, then," he said. And we switched places. I was furious and knew I was right so, a few minutes later, I jumped overboard and swam to shore. Father and Jeff rowed after me to the beach. I thought of the discomfort and shame of walking home in my wet clothes, so I got back into the passenger's seat. But when we reached the family float, I managed to get out first. Then, when Father stood on the float, I held out my hand as a gesture of apology and pushed him backwards into the water. He went down like a stone and I will never forget the surprise on his face as he popped up again. His hat was still on his head but had turned around 180 degrees. Jeffy looked shocked but Father and I both burst out laughing. The battle was over.

As a student-adventurer, I often felt I was at Father's mercy. The experience of the snake on the path when I was eight was echoed many years later when Father led me and Hugh Scott, a college boyfriend, on a trek in Spain's Costa Brava. Night fell and still we walked on into the unknown, winding up at an army encampment where the soldiers showed us the way to town. I was so tired and so angry that I rushed on ahead through the dark, feeling the path through my sneakers. I don't think I spoke to Father until the next morning, when the three of us pressed on in a hired boat to a Carthaginian ruin in the town of Ampurias.

Hugh was still with us when, after another long day, on our way to a very belated supper in Avignon, I turned and kicked Father's shin. There was a sort of inaudible gasp from the French families drinking aperitifs at the sidewalk cafes. But Father and I, I think, were both quite pleased with ourselves as we finally entered the restaurant and ordered an excellent meal. Hugh departed the next day. Father and I enjoyed these tiffs and they reinforced my own sense that it was safe to disagree with the boss. For him, they added spice to life.

Reefing the boat's stiff canvas in the midst of a gale was hard work and I was terrified of setting a spinnaker with its heavy pole and the need for split-second timing. These days I don't go out by myself in the knockabout. After various frights and bangs, and with the growing frailties of age, I have become more timid. Still, I think of Father each time I go out in a boat, or when I face just one more bend in an unknown road ahead. I think of the long hot noons drifting in sunbaked calm, of the dreamlike winds of the morning and the afternoon blasts. I think of anchoring in some tiny deserted cove and going ashore to walk or pick shellfish for supper, of the soft nights with all of us talking and eating on deck or under a kerosene lamp down below.

And I think of the fun we had together and the skills I learned that have applied to so many other aspects of life. Without Father, I would never have learned to eat sea urchins' eggs, to see the magic of Conrad and Trollope and Yeats, or to measure danger by the sound of waves on the shore or the sudden shift of somebody's voice, urgently warning, urging me on.

Chapter 10

Rosamond

Four years had passed since Mother's death; the war had ended and my father had been back in our old house in Brookline for a year when he encountered the woman who became our first stepmother.

Rosamond Forbes Bowers, the daughter of Father's friend and painting mentor, Edward Forbes, must have captivated him from the moment he saw her walking toward him near Naushon's Stone House that summer afternoon in 1947. Dark and willowy, Ros was the oldest of four children. Her first marriage had taken her to Seattle and, following her divorce, she had stayed on the West Coast. So we hardly knew her.

Father, again at Harvard though still commuting to Woods Hole for the old war project, must have talked about her. But there is no mention of her in his letters until that fall. Then he wrote to me at boarding school that he had received a letter and a book on Jung from Ros, who had returned to California. "I wish she were not so entangled with all that Jungian analysis," the letter says, "but perhaps

Ros Forbes, Jeffries' second wife, mid-1940s. (Photographer unknown.)

it is good for her . . . Ros is a most loveable person and has written me two delightful letters."

My own schoolgirlish designs on my widowed father were clear from the draft of a letter I had sent to Aunt Susan that spring. In it I proposed that, instead of going back to a music camp, I should spend the summer in Brookline. I argued that I could get a job taking care of rabbits in a Harvard lab or working in a greenhouse. It would be nice for Father to have at least one family member around as he resettled into the house. Besides, he and I weren't getting along very well. "I would like him to think of me as a companion and not as a little girl," I wrote. "This would be a perfect chance to devote my time to him because everyone else would be away. It would be fun to get up together and cook breakfast together and then drive to work together etc." My last pitch was that Father might teach me Greek.

Needless to say, I spent the summer at the music camp, where I played the violin and later the viola. Jeffy was working at a boatyard and living with Aunt Susan in Marblehead, where I joined him when camp was over. I was seventeen and Jeffy a year younger.

As it turned out, Father and Ros were married on January 21, 1948. Jeffy and I were taken completely by surprise. Even Ros seemed startled. "A week ago we were married," she wrote me, "and it all seems quite like a miracle. To me it is one—everything from last summer on." They honeymooned in a borrowed cabin somewhere near Wilmington, Vermont, where, she wrote, "the temperature away from the fire in the room where we sit is usually between 20 and 30 degrees!"

Only a few weeks earlier I had staged a music house party in the Stone House for about a dozen young musicians. We played Beethoven quartets in front of the parlor fire and ice hockey, with a lump of wood as the puck, on the pond near the Naushon Farm. Father and Jeff had both been there but there had been no mention of Father's marriage plans. A letter from Jeffy to me, dated February 9, refers to the party but makes no mention at all of Ros. When the wedding took place, she was thirty-nine and Father was forty-six.

···

Two years after Father's death, I went to visit Ros at the old farmhouse outside Boston she had shared with her third husband, Carl Pickhardt, for more than forty years. Now she was eighty-nine. Her face was wrinkled and her clothes baggy but she still had warmth and style. I'd brought her eight pink roses, and she took me through the house to a cold storeroom where she found a vase and we cut the stems together. Then we settled in the parlor, she beside an unlit fire and I on a strange sofa that turned out to be three faintly art-deco chairs placed side by side. They reminded me of her orange-crate side tables in Cambridge.

Even though I had seen her very little in the preceding decades, we had no trouble discussing the past. Ros told me she had known my mother at Radcliffe and had liked her rich laughter and refreshing personality. Father, too, had been part of the Cambridge scene. At first, Ros said, she found him "offish and a wet blanket." But after his marriage to my mother she became "enchanted" with this man who told her that her wandering thoughts reminded him of Laurence Sterne's novel *Tristram Shandy*.

Ros told me—to my amazement and awe—that following her divorce from Bill Bowers she had lived for two years with a younger woman. That "wonderful but stormy" relationship was breaking up and she was feeling anguished when she met my father. Theirs was "a glamorous courtship," she recalled. Father had come often to her family's summer house, facing Vineyard Sound from Naushon. They would sail to some offshore islands or ride horses to a remote beach and swim without bathing suits. He came to the fall roundup of sheep on the neighboring island of Nashawena. They exchanged their first kiss on the big rock on the hill overlooking Quick's Hole.

Ros returned to Berkeley in the autumn and immediately got a letter from Father asking her to marry him. By Thanksgiving she was back in Cambridge, living at her family's house. Father would often stop by on his way home from Harvard. Heads would pop out the doors as he climbed to her third-floor rooms. There was no privacy, Ros told me, and she was still in a turmoil about her life. She was shocked when she learned that on New Year's Day Father had told my mother's family that he was going to marry her.

She had been warned that my parents were intellectual snobs, so lofty that "they left their children behind." Ros desperately wanted to have children of her own but Father adamantly refused. He had two children already and that was enough, he insisted. She had been told that Father was "bad with money and very difficult"; leaving the lights blazing in an empty room was a sin. But, in spite of her doubts, Ros agreed to the marriage.

"I was hopelessly in love with Jeff," she recalled with characteristic candor. "The passion between us was always good. I loved his voice; it was so beautiful. Physically, he was my image of a lover as no one had been before."

This disclosure was news to me. The idea of my father as a Romeo seemed totally out of character. Never a prude, he had seemed to treat sex as a good and natural thing, a force that inspired poems and jokes, a matter of interest and good manners, but not a major concern in his life.

I asked Ros about Father's earlier romance with her cousin Ruth, an artist, twice married already and the mother of two teenaged sons. "Oh yes," Ros said cheerfully. "They were lovers for a long time. They used to meet under the big oak on Goat's Neck." I felt chagrined that, despite my vigilance, I had missed this chapter in my father's life. But I remembered noticing that, in a letter as far back as 1944, Father had written about a long walk with Ruth on Naushon and had stopped to decorate the "R" in her name as he thought about her as a partner. Ruth had backed out, Ros said, when she saw Jeffries with his children, "putting you down, shoving you around and then being relaxed and happy."

This hot-and-cold tendency was to doom his new marriage. And my own ambivalence about Ros's claims of love and motherhood didn't help. When she moved into the Brookline house, Ros wanted to make it her own. In February, a month after the wedding, she wrote me that she planned to convert our old nursery into her study and dressing room. "We are going to make it a modern room with a door through to Jeffries' study, which will be our bedroom, I think."

Even now, after fifty years, I can feel my hackles rise at these proposals. The nursery where we'd tried to trap sunlight in a shoebox, where our young cook had played "Red Sails in the Sunset" on the upright piano, where Jeff and I had eaten Sunday supper in front of a coal grate, all would be utterly ruined. But Jeffy and I, both off at school and desperately anxious to keep in touch with Father, had no standing in the matter. Father initially seemed to accept the changes without comment.

Ros's plans never came off, however. By May, she was writing to me about moving to the little house that she owned next door to her parents in Cambridge. "I find this [Brookline] house is so much his house that I can't manage to find my part in it . . . Does it mean a great deal to you?" Well, of course it did! Until Mother's death in 1943, our whole family life had been there. But perhaps I didn't dare to say so.

Then, in June, Father announced that they would be in Ros's house "for a time this autumn, but not all winter as it is too small really for you to have your own rooms there."

By then I sensed considerable pressure on Father's part to keep us out of town.

It was arranged that I should spend the summer on a cousin's ranch in Sheridan, Wyoming, while Jeff was sent off to sea on the Oceanographic research vessel, *Atlantis*. Father was pressing my brother, who had transferred to the Brooks School north of Boston, to take a postgraduate year as a boarder at Milton Academy, rather than accept admission to some "third-rate small college." I had been accepted at Radcliffe, Stanford, and McGill University in Montreal. "The idea of you and Jeffy living at home seems to be out," Father wrote, "and my advice to you is to go to McGill. You could later change to Radcliffe if you wanted to."

Ros, meanwhile, was dutifully trying to be a good wife and mother. She went with Father to dinners all over town and met his friends and relations, who, since Father had almost no family, were mostly connections of my mother's. She planned a skiing vacation in

March for Jeffy and went with Father on a parental visit to Brooks, only to learn that Jeff was racing with the school crew on the Charles River in Cambridge. They returned in time to see his boat lose the race. She also became immersed in plans for my graduation from Baldwin on June 8 and the coming debutante season: planning a dinner party in my honor before a dance and writing endless letters about the date, the location of the party and the guests.

Facing all this upheaval, Father behaved as I would learn he always did when confronted with family stress. He arranged to disappear. He accepted an invitation to spend three weeks in England, where he would speak at a scientific conference in Cambridge and visit friends. He departed on June 5, less than six months into his marriage and three days before my school graduation. A Forbes relation acted as his stand-in at the debutante dinner the following week.

Neither of them, I think, had any idea that Jeffy and I would feel uncomfortable with all this outside intervention. Sometimes it could be absurd. I still remember being sent off to Boston's annual Cotillion with a necklace lent me by Ros that looked like an exploding ruff of small Christmas balls. I stood in the ladies' room before the music started, wondering what to do with it. It was too precious to lose, too big to hide.

I put the bauble in my coat pocket. But I felt like a wallflower.

···

By summer, the marriage was already on shaky ground. They had spent several weeks together on the remote island of Nashawena, a time that Father described as "good but difficult in many ways, for Ros is so sensitive and high-strung." He seems to have been trying to smooth things over. He wrote of cooking "thin pancakes with chopped beef and a spinach sauce" and went on to describe preparations for the move to Cambridge in the fall. Then, in August it was

Ros's turn to leave. She went back to her Jungian institute in California and was away until September.

She was there and I was back in Brookline when she sent me a letter saying, "I gather from something that Jeff wrote that you are feeling critical of me. Please remember that no one can understand all the elements and problems and tasks of another person's life and try not to make judgments. Know that I love Jeff, that I love you and Jeffy, and that in being here now I am doing what is most necessary for me to become more alive and creative in our family life as well as in my own living."

Now I can sympathize with Ros, but then I found her words just mawkish. Very much my father's daughter, I was embarrassed by her emotional outpourings. Father believed in getting on with life; Ros believed in bathing in it.

By September 1948, tenants had once again moved into our Brookline house and Father and Ros were in Cambridge. On October 2 he wrote me at McGill: "Ros is radiantly happy in her house and I must say in many ways it is quite pleasant. But I don't like living in Cambridge. I feel at the moment rather rebellious about life in general. I want to finish the book Dr. [John] Edsall and I are writing but my mind craves the outdoors and aesthetic things more and more rather than academic ones. However the spell of abstract ideas still holds me. In my next reincarnation I should like best (or so I feel now) to be either a pure mathematician or an artist. I miss you very much and wish we could have a good long walk together and talk about everything." The allure to me of such a letter was almost irresistible. And, when I was around, we did walk and talk but, as I recall, our conversation was mostly about ideas and future plans.

I was setting off for Europe on my own after my freshman year in Montreal. Father was helping with plans and money. "Understand," he wrote in January 1949, "I want you to go and am delighted that you have the gumption to make all the arrangements. How much is it going to cost and how much are you going to be able to contribute from your allowance?" The same letter revealed that he was reading *The Tale of Genji* and painting watercolors in his time off from Harvard. The marriage seemed to be going more smoothly. And Ros wrote in March to say that "for me the critical time is over."

The calm did not last. Rediscovering these letters now, I can see that the split was almost inevitable. Father and Ros wanted things to work out but they came at it from totally opposite poles. That April of 1949 they went with Ros's uncle, Alexander Forbes, to northern Vermont for four days. "I enjoyed it greatly," Father wrote, "but I fear Ros could not. We stayed in a camp way up on the mountain & in the woods at 2,700 feet. She was much oppressed by the trees and also by the materialistic outlook of Alex and me."

Soon after that, Ros went to New York for a week. "It will be good, I think, for Jeff and me to have a little vacation," she wrote. "We have been having some rough weather for a bit. That does not affect what I said to you about you for me, if you see what I mean." I didn't see what she meant, and still don't. Upon her return, Father went to collect her and to meet her psychiatrist but found Ros "very depressed." He felt her continued contact with her former lover, Mary, who had married and moved East, just made things worse but admitted, "I am not responsive enough to her very expressive and demonstrative affectionate nature."

I sailed for Europe on May 24. On Memorial Day, with Ros again absent, Father and Jeffy returned to Vermont. "We found a nice wood road by a brook where we spent the night. We were as warm as you please in our sleeping bags and were up and away walking by six next morning." Ros had returned by the time they got back and the same day wrote to me in London, "I have told Jeff that I have to be alone this summer." She wanted to work on a project about African tribes and had copied "another Bushman painting of blue and black ostriches." I had moved on to an Austrian summer school in the Tyrol and it was a month before I got her letter.

Jeffy turned down Father's offer of a cruise in Maine followed by a summer at a lumber camp belonging to his college friend Carl Weyerhaeuser, and instead drove out West with school friends to work on the wheat harvest. So Father went on his own to Maine and spent the rest of the summer painting in Nova Scotia. When my homebound ship reached port in late August I found a letter from Ros. It said, "I am having to face the fact that I can not live with Jeff."

Within a month Father had moved into the third-floor apartment in Will Forbes's house in Milton, where Jeffy and I joined him. Ros continued to see him; in fact their relationship blossomed when they were apart. But by September the marriage of twenty-one months was over.

→••→

During my visit those many years later, Ros and I had talked for two hours when Carl returned from the fishing club where he went each morning and occasionally met my brother, Jeff. We sat down to a lunch of three frozen chicken pot pies and homemade tomato aspic molded in empty tin cans. A week after our talk, Ros sent me two photographs. They were of a beautiful unworried young woman; the dates 1946 and 1947 were penciled on the backs. It seemed impossible that they could have been taken when she was nearly forty, just before she married Father.

The whole thing seems touching and funny now. But it hadn't always felt that way. Had Ros never realized how angry I was with them both? "No," she said as I prepared to leave. "I loved you very much. You were my true standby at that time." And she told me with pleasure and affection that I had once written her that "Father deserves a kick in the pants and you need a sedative." How could she miss the rage, even now? There had been no family; she was not our mother; and I couldn't intervene because my father had been in love with her.

During our long talk, Ros showed me two letters from my father, written from Paris, years after their divorce. One was dated 1984, when Father, by then married to Olga Lodigensky, had been reflecting on an autobiographical article. "My life," he wrote, "has been blessed by three remarkable wives, each as different and as important in making me what I am as the primary colors are in vision. Although this is too personal for a scientific autobiography, I wanted you to know how I feel. With love, Jeff. P.S. I cannot say what color belongs to which wife."

The other, written in January 1990, in the tiny shaking hand of his Parkinson's disease, says "Dear Ros, Thank you for your letter which brought to mind so many precious things. Do you remember what I once said to you of my three wives? It is still true! But writing is so difficult for me that I will say no more."

"Jeff was a complete joy if you weren't in intimacy with him," Ros said as I gave her a farewell hug.

Ros died on October 12, 2004, two days before her ninety-sixth birthday. Her third husband, the painter, Carl Pickhardt, died in a nearby nursing home four weeks later. As many people said at the small service in their Sherborn farmhouse, "Ros hated to let people go."

Chapter 11

Japan

The urge to travel was part of my father's New England heritage. ✓
And now, as after my mother's death, and following his divorce
from Ros, it was triggered by a double loss.

Following his separation from Ros, he spent several months in a
rather frantic, unhappy round of dinner parties. There were evenings
at Boston's Tavern Club, afternoons chopping trees with Amory
Coolidge in Westwood and visits to a Cabot family house in Walpole,
New Hampshire, "where," he wrote, "life seems so warm and harmless." Even his work at Harvard seemed stale, with middle-aged
Harvard colleagues whom he found "drab, dull and disappointing."

An invitation to give a series of scientific lectures in Korea came
like a rescue.

He never got to his destination. North Korean forces invaded the
Republic of South Korea on June 25, 1950. When the attack was
announced, Father, already en route by air, was at a stopover in the
Aleutian Islands. Unfazed, he continued to Tokyo and, through General Douglas MacArthur's aide-de-camp, Laurence Bunker, arranged
to transfer his program of lectures to universities throughout Japan
for the next six months.

Five years after the end of World War II Japan was being rebuilt by the United States. Father was forty-nine and he had a life and vocation behind him. Science, art and outdoor adventure were hotly smoldering interests, and all fanned to flame as he got closer and closer to Japanese culture.

Now, with his government's imprimatur, he was treated as a royal guest. Armed with early white hair and the bearing of a sea captain, Father would sail through the world like a Victorian prince for the rest of his life. This was true whether he was in a remote village or in a busy city. Natives in huts came up to touch him as he lay in their best hammock. Counts and colonels, whose titles and ancestry he always recorded, entertained him at elaborate dinners. He would pass this off in his letters, saying, "but of course I don't care for all this!" An obvious lie.

Unlike his own grandfather, who journeyed primarily for science, and unlike his father, who hoped to win manhood on the railroads in Nebraska, Father seems to have sought a world of his imagination, partly gleaned from the old books of his boyhood and partly from his own ideas of what the world should be. Amazingly, people responded to his vision in a way that would seem impossible today.

In 1950 members of MacArthur's staff surmised that, beyond his usefulness in bringing modern science to Japan's reemerging academy, Father could be a kind of eccentric ambassador in the countryside. He also had connections of his own and used one to lead to another. Bearing an introduction from Harvard's Langdon Warner, who was credited with saving Kyoto from American bombing, Father was invited to the Imperial Palace the day after his arrival in Tokyo on June 28. He found Emperor Hirohito, an amateur marine biologist, "a simple and delightful man." The Marquis of Matsudira, the Emperor's grand master of ceremonies, became a personal friend.

Father in Japan, in 1950, during his round of lectures there during the Korean War.
(Photographer unknown.)

Days later Father attended a fisheries meeting on the Pacific coast with an American official, recorded only as Mr. Herrington. They met the local fisheries team at a small country inn. Father described the event with zest and a presumptuous tone of authority. More than ever he was chronicling his adventures in lengthy letters home that served as a personal diary. Jeff and I were obviously expected to be the keepers of the flame.

"Tea was served and the discussion went on and on, each English statement by Herrington seeming to expand into an oration by the interpreter," he wrote. "They were fine looking men on the whole, hard and brown beyond the usual brown of a Japanese. When at last it was over, we had the usual Japanese bath, put on yukatas (a kind of kimono) and were ready for the banquet which was given for us by the fishermen . . . There was much hilariousness and all the dead seriousness of the discussion was gone. The girls in their kimonos, according to custom, came and kneeled close to us and filled our glasses as we ate. Sometimes they would take us by the hand or arm. There were all sorts of different fish dishes, both raw and cooked. At the end of the meal, one of the old men, a mayor of a nearby village, got up and did a kind of rowing dance as the others sang and clapped. Then I was made to get up and dance with one of the girls. After it was all over, [Herrington and I] went to a room upstairs where tea was brought. We could hear the rote of the sea on the beach 500 yards away and the screens were pulled aside so that cool breezes blew through the room."

Soon he managed to escape the military bureaucracy and was adventuring virtually on his own. The possibility of danger and discomfort was part of the allure. Every professional visit to an outlying university was enhanced with visits to wild places. In late July he was nearly caught by night on an eighteen-mile hike over the remote Akan Mountains in Hokkaido, guided by a football player from

Sapporo University and a local forester who carried a gun to ward off bears on the trail.

Everywhere his Japanese contacts appeared delighted to learn that Father's real interest was in the art and ancient culture of their country. Academics would abandon their labs and offices to take him off to see some ancient house, some beautiful piece of land-scape, some craftsmen or workers skilled in old ways. In the process, perhaps his hosts had a chance to recapture the traditions they were losing after the war. Certainly the inscrutable mask gave way to real hospitality in the face of his enthusiasm.

A young biochemist named Yoshiaki Miura invited him to visit his wife's family at their country estate near Nasu. During a swimming picnic, Father was amazed to see Miura's noble father-in-law swept down the river past workers who were building a dam. The old Count emerged unscathed and the family returned to the house, where Father was called on to advise the Count's farmers about birth control.

Another Japanese friend was Kyoshi Kurahashi, then twenty-eight and also a biochemist in Tokyo. He was with Father during a September typhoon in Nara when a tree fell onto their charcoal-fueled taxi, destroying the engine and collapsing the roof over Father's head. Father and Kurahashi abandoned the poor taximan, continued their shrine-viewing on foot and, the next day, climbed through the rain to a sacred lake where they spent the night on the floor of a deserted hostel. Back in Tokyo, he went to Kurahashi's house to read *Hamlet* with Kyoshi and his brother, who had studied drama at the University of Washington State. (After Father's death, Professor Kurahashi wrote me that he, himself, "sweated" over the part of Ophelia.)

An older companion was Ichiro Mizushima, who, at the age of forty, was a professor of physical chemistry at Tokyo University and director of the Institute of Science and Technology at Komba. Mizushima knew everyone of consequence and helped Father to meet them, providing entree to private collections of art, taking him to the top of Mount Fuji and whisking him off from his Tokyo lectures to two-hour dinners complete with geishas.

My father's six months in Japan were like a tumultuous love affair. On September 24 he wrote Jeff and me, "I have never been given so much attention in my life and Miura thinks it exceeds that given to any visiting scholar in Japan he has heard of. It is all due to a combination of things." The letter rushes on without explaining the "things," but I can only conclude the acclaim was due not only to Father's government standing, but to his extraordinary vigor, his omnivorous interests and his passion to understand everything Japanese.

The letter concludes with a long encomium to Japan that starts out, "My great lament is the loss of old traditions by the Japanese in their pursuit of our shoddy ways . . . In my opinion it is closely connected with the loss of respect and reverence and a sense of religion, and the corresponding growth of casualness, individualism and egoism which is spreading from the West." He goes on to condemn "certain absurd material comforts like bathrooms, effortless transportation by wheels, overheated rooms, food available without any effort at a minute's notice, shows we can take in passively without the need of imagination or understanding . . . We in the West think of human enterprises as justified by their effect on the material life of the community. Actually, as the East well knows, nothing could be farther from the truth."

Even science comes in for criticism. "Science," he wrote, "is valuable because of the wonderful philosophical picture it has given us, as in biology and physics and mathematics. It has made us conceptually richer and, in that role, it belongs to the arts and is the primary adornment of modern life. But because of its material effects, it has been a source of evil and disintegration."

While I took this Jovian view of modern civilization at face value and was annoyed at its pomposity then, it now seems loveable and absurd. The American Indians were happy to replace their stick sleds or "travois" with wheels. Father, who often ate an instant lunch of cold rice on his walks, did not prepare a single meal for himself in Japan. And surely the gifts of health and knowledge obtained through science are not entirely evil. "I have written too much and incoherently but I feel very strongly," he admits. But what a romantic vision!

Near the end of his visit, in November, he and his friend Kurahashi were traveling by motorized boat up the Kumano River on the Kii Peninsula, southeast of Osaka. "On the way up the tributary," he wrote, "we came upon a very beautiful sight, all the more so from being encountered in that wild mountain setting. It was a fleet of river boats under sail trying to make their way against the current before a leading wind . . . They were strange and beautiful things, rather more like birds than boats, or, at any rate, like some kind of river beings. I was deeply humiliated at doing them the indignity of passing them in the propeller boat . . . I left them with the same feelings with which I might have passed a company of nymphs."

My father's style of travel was modeled after his grandfather's. In 1858, following sojourns in Paris, Labrador and Surinam related to his study of anatomy, the first of the four Jeffries Wymans had made an eight months' journey to South America with Robert Bennet Forbes, William G. Saltonstall and George Augustus Peabody. The party of four left Boston on November 18 in bad weather. On the fifth day out Forbes's brig, which carried a coal-burning vessel of fifty-two by thirteen feet on deck, was dismasted. But the crew borrowed a spar from a northbound ship and reached Montevideo in eight weeks. On the way south my ancestor had collected marine organisms and dissected a porpoise and—while his companions explored the Rio Plata, hunted game and paid social calls in Uruguay—my great-grandfather reconnoitered for science. In April, Forbes went home, sending the brig on to China. The other three set out in a horse-drawn wagon for the Pacific coast, crossing the Andes on horseback. The first Jeffries, who willingly put up with noise, dirt and fleas, was unused to riding and was thrown off his mount when he put up an umbrella at the foot of the Cordillera. Later he slipped backward over his horse's tail when the girth broke on a steep pass. But the trio reached Chile, caught a steamer for Panama and eventually got back to Boston.

In contrast, my grandfather, after driving a train through a line of striking railway workers in Alliance, Nebraska, never really left New England again.

My brother, who is a world-class angler, is not a world-class traveler either. He has fished for salmon in Siberia and, in 1958, made a long trip through the Sudan with my father. But, other than occasional trips to Europe, Jeff's journeys mostly take him now to a Florida backwater called Chuckaluski, where he and a famous guide, Gil Drake, stay in a shabby motel and fish the mangrove swamps for snook and permit.

I was a better disciple. That wild walk on the Costa Brava when I was just out of college was my first long trip with my father. It taught me to expect and even to enjoy the unexpected. In 1961 Father and I spent ten days paddling a kayak through the lakes of eastern Finland, stopping at farmhouses along the shore. One mid-August night after supper, a boy came and led us, almost blindfolded, through dark root-studded spruce woods to the island home of an old poet who had heard of our presence. He had a radio in his dark rooms and

*Jeffries Wyman and daughter Anne with a family they visited in Finland in August
1961, where they learned of the construction of the Berlin Wall.
(Photographed by a member of the host family; collection of the author.)*

spoke English. That day, he told us, the Russians had started building
a wall dividing Berlin.

Our last trip together came in 1973, when Father persuaded a forest ranger, whose son-in-law was a fellow scientist, to include me on
a pack trip along the middle fork of Idaho's Salmon River. The
ranger brought an old friend and the three men slept in a big tent
while I lodged in a pup tent nearby. But I got used to the horses skid-
ding around hairpin turns, learned to throw a diamond hitch and
played the harmonica when it got lonesome.

By then I had completed five years as the *Boston Globe*'s first in-
house travel writer. The paper had previously relied on freelance

writers, and because it had never before had such a slot, I was pretty much able to write my own ticket and go wherever I chose. And being a woman proved a help rather than a hindrance. Between 1965 and 1970 I visited forty-one countries, eighteen states and fourteen Caribbean islands. My father's inside-out mode of travel, which I adopted, prevailed over the advertising department's interest in cities where tourists would go and spend money. I was lucky and the section grew as I wrote oddball stories about fishing in Labrador, bird-watching in Iceland and Soviet sailing clubs on the Black Sea. Father's adventures were always on my mind and, after he could no longer travel, I felt I could explore on his behalf. I remember how excited he was to hear about my trip to Vietnam the year before he died. And, looking back, it's striking how closely I followed my father's trail.

My first trip for the *Globe* was to Guatemala, where I spent a Thanksgiving walking in the hills past Indians on their way to market and where I learned that the best guides are fearless small boys who speak the language, will go anywhere, and know the way home. Like Father, I went to northern Thailand, where I sat on the floor and watched a dance put on for Burmese generals who had come over the border, perhaps to smuggle opium from the nearby hills. On a cruise that wound up in Port Moresby, New Guinea, I visited the art museum and saw wonderful carvings like those my father had seen in the back country when he visited there years before. I even got to Japan, where I met his old friend, Mizushima.

Also like Father, I took chances and could never forgo looking around the next bend in the road. Once, on a brambly track in Hawaii, I was frightened by headlights in my rearview mirror. They turned out to be the reflection of my own taillights on a wreck abandoned in the bushes. Once in the Caribbean I went out to view remote hotels in a skiff with three local men who offered me their bottle of rum and a rope-tow behind the boat. They seemed in no

As a travel editor of the Boston Globe *in the 1960s, the author, already a licensed
private-plane pilot, flies as a guest pilot with the Blue Angels.
(Photo by Paul J. Connell; © 1964 Globe Newspaper Company. Reprinted
with permission.)*

hurry to get me to my departing plane. Miss Dinsey, who kept the
tiny hotel in town, packed my things and met me at the dock with a
taxi.

But on the whole, I was a sissy compared to my father. In Sapporo to preview the Winter Olympics of 1972, I had a Japanese-style
massage instead of climbing the mountains. On Kyushu, I wrote
about the aquarium and honeymoon couples instead of visiting an
ancient pottery works. My only exciting boat ride in Japan, where
Father had had so many, was crossing the Inland Sea on a steamer
with a man who carried a revolver in his briefcase. Thinking of
Father, I pretended I hadn't seen the gun. Now I wonder if my fellow
traveler could have been a policeman. Father would have thought I
was silly to worry.

Chapter 12

Painting

Father's six months in Japan in 1950 and his journey home by way of Bangkok, Calcutta, Istanbul and London had given him a taste of freedom. His next five months back at Harvard gave him the taste of a prison.

He found his colleagues dull and was bored with life in the city. So, in the summer of 1951, Father again took off from Harvard to attend an academic meeting in Colorado. As usual, though, his real goal was to visit a wild place where a handful of people lived in traditional ways in harmony with the natural world around them. It was in places such as this that the artist in him could best flourish. Painting was another of Father's ways to escape.

Happily, he was able to arrange to spend a few weeks at Anaktuvuk, a tiny weather station in Alaska's remote Brooks Range. His old acquaintance Terris Moore, then the president of the University of Alaska in Fairbanks, flew him north in his seaplane. Father's detailed journal describes a false start when the plane failed to get off the water and he waded ashore, holding his watch high out of reach of the waves. But they eventually made it and Father, with the big yellow canvas painting bag that he had sewed himself, filled with brushes, paints and watercolor paper, said farewell to Moore and settled in for the month of August with the fifty-six-year-old Elijah Kakina and two other Nunamiut Eskimo families. Although it was late summer, the weather could be quirky. Snow and harsh winds were frequent.

The big skin tents where these families lived were clustered on the open tundra with the mountains of Anaktuvuk Pass not far away. Father slept with Elijah and his family in piles of wolf and caribou fur. He ate caribou or sheep from animals that the men sighted with ancient telescopes steadied on forked sticks. All of this figured in a series of beautiful cobalt and sepia watercolors of the landscape and—for almost the only time in his painting life—of the people he lived with. I have those paintings now in my house in Cambridge. There is a beautiful portrait of Elijah, in his blue parka with its dark fur ruff, gazing slightly downward as if his mind is far away. Elijah's short black hair is ruffled and his grizzled face is serene. Over my bed, a woman sits against a pile of furs, holding a little boy between her legs. Elijah's ten-year-old grandson, Raymond, is the subject of a separate portrait. He leans forward from his furry nest, hands on his knees as if he were anxious to be off on an expedition. Another painting shows the silhouette of a girl playing cat's cradle against the doorway of the tent.

It turned out that while in Colorado my father had contracted Rocky Mountain Spotted Fever so, although he sometimes helped Elijah and others to pull fish nets, follow caribou hunts and string traps for ground squirrels (whose livers he found to be a delicacy), he often stayed close to the camp, writing and painting. As always, during his thirty-one days in Alaska he kept a diary which, transcribed later, came to 150 double-spaced typewritten pages. During that time he also produced over 100 drawings and watercolors.

May made Father a pair of skin mukluks and a wolf-fur ruff for his parka. "Walking on the tundra is almost like walking on sand," he wrote in his diary. And the sealskin-soled mukluks with their oiled caribou leggings were "waterproof to the upper part of the calves, very warm and delightfully comfortable. It gives me a great feeling of independence to jump out of a boat into 8 or 10 inches of water without a thought and run [the boat] up on the shore." The wolf fur, which doesn't freeze with your breath, protected him from winds that could blow at fifty miles per hour.

One day, he related in his diary, the men made a long expedition to hunt ground squirrels. Father took his paints and spent most of the day painting while the others checked their traps. It was ten hours before they got back to camp, cold, wet—and, in Father's case, feverish. On another occasion, Father watched as Elijah, with his grandson Raymond and one of the other men in the settlement, shot three male caribou. They brought back 1,000 pounds of meat for storage in a well dug deep into the permafrost. A young woman gave him the quill of a golden eagle, which he used in writing his diary, and a little ground squirrel bag, which he used to hold his quills and pencils. Simon, who manned the weather station with Elijah, was making him a skin model of a kayak; Father followed its progress in pencil and paper in hopes of making a full-sized model back home.

Another evening, Father put on his warmest things and went out to do a watercolor of the hills, Simon's tent and two children. "I found it quite beyond my powers as usual to express what I wanted but had a delightful & absorbingly interesting time," he wrote. ". . . The evenings are on the whole the most beautiful & exciting time for outdoor painting. But it is always cold & things change in the flash of an eye. Finished my painting about 10 when it is now getting too dark to see colors well. During the course of it, the children were romping and playing in all quarters and came every so often to look on. The most primitive satisfaction provided by a picture to the observer is, I suppose, the act of identification and children love to see a picture underway and be able to exclaim, 'That is the door of Simon's house; that is the old caribou skin,' etc. It is an important, though lower, aspect of art which, it seems to me, is too little present in modern pictures."

On August 16 it was snowing outside the tents. Father stayed inside and painted the watercolor of Raymond in his best new caribou parka, sitting on a pile of furs. While out looking in vain for caribou, Elijah shot five ptarmigan. "I am constantly reminded of Mary Cassatt in the scenes of children and mothers," he wrote. "She combined something of abstractness, formality and the style of the [Japanese] ukiyo-e, with all the tenderness of a woman towards children, and she never became sentimental." Father himself refused to be sentimental about painting victims of the Eskimo hunts. One day, after watching a caribou escape, he noted that "the thought of the wounded animal as a prey to wolves is not pleasant." Still, he sat on the tundra to paint a fresh carcass while Elijah skinned two others nearby, and described it as "a wonderful subject." The next morning he set out to paint the piles of meat left on the hillside to await transport by the dogs.

Father's painting life had begun as a boy in Gloucester when he took lessons from an old man who lived nearby. He did a few oils in Austria during the summer he was there with John Edsall, in their student years. And I think there were some attempts with my mother when we were children. But it was Ros's father, Edward Forbes, who really got Father going, hitching up a horse and carriage and taking him on painting picnics on Naushon, and showing him the treasures of Harvard's Fogg Museum, where Forbes was the director from 1909 to 1944 and brought new life to a dead collection.

Once hooked on painting he made it an integral part of his life.

One Christmas my brother and I unearthed a stack of Father's watercolors from the cellar and figured out that he had done over 100 paintings in the year 1948 alone, including several views of the oil tanks lining the upper reaches of Boston Harbor. When we were at North Haven he carried his paints everywhere, going off in the rowboat along the shore, or through the woods to a picnic site where he would paint while Jeff and I dozed after lunch. He painted from our Fisher's Island sloop when we were cruising and, one morning when I jumped overboard for a swim in the freezing Maine water and couldn't get back on the sloop, I discovered Father had taken the tender ashore and was sketching on the far side of the little island, unable to hear my shouts. Even when we once ran aground in the *Kestrel*, Father found an opportunity to paint a picture of our stranding.

He spent a great deal of time looking at art, too. When Jeffy and I were little, Father and Mother often took us to the Isabella Stewart Gardner Museum and to Boston's Museum of Fine Arts, where Edward Forbes was also a trustee. The Gardner, which preserved the collection of a rich and eccentric Boston lady, was fun because of the beautiful courtyard and the furnishings. But for us the M.F.A. had more treasures. There was the picture by John Singleton Copley of "Watson," being eaten by a shark, his hair streaming one way and blood from his leg streaming the other, as the crew of a dory, which includes a black man, looks on in horror. And there was George Washington, painted by Gilbert Stuart, with his hand on the rump of his retreating horse. Once, during a show of classical art, I was enthralled by Pieter Brueghel's tiny oil painting from Brussels showing Icarus falling into the sea while a farmer on a bright sunny headland goes on ploughing his fields. Upstairs overlooking Huntington Avenue, we would fold back the silk cloth on a very long table and marvel at the twelfth-century saga of "The Burning of Sanjo Palace" before going down to visit the Zen garden with its surrounding gallery of Japanese actors and warriors. For Father and Jeff there were the mummies and sarcophaguses. For Mother and me there were the tiny cabinets containing lighted models of early New England rooms.

Nowadays, as a treat, my brother and I meet every month or so for a viewing and lunch at the M.F.A. But the Zen garden is now out of doors, and "The Burning of Sanjo Palace" has been rolled up and stored away, along with many of the Japanese warriors.

Painting had also formed a close bond with Ros. They were at the Forbes island of Nashawena in the first year of their marriage when Father wrote, "I made lots of bread and painted several pictures. Ros has given me a fine set of watercolors & I mean to try some larger pictures here." That fall Ros wrote to me at college that she had seen Father's "array of paintings. He has done some very beautiful things and the whole accomplishment is very great, I think ... I am very thrilled with his painting and his excitement over it."

That November he and Ros drove down to Pigeon Cove, near Rockport, and Father painted two pictures, "one a complete failure and the other, painted at the last minute just as the sun was going down, quite a success." In January, after doing three other paintings, he wrote that "the last [is] the best and I am quite pleased with it, though it suffers from being too pretty." I never thought his paintings were just "pretty." To me they combine dash and robustness with real skill and a feeling for nature. An offshore rock surrounded by ripples moves with the waves; a huge country house in France makes you wonder what goes on behind its blank windows. Elijah and his children in Anaktuvuk look at the viewer with trust and the knowledge that soon he will be gone. For me, these are permanent records of someone who lived in the moment.

When his marriage to Ros was in trouble in 1949, he took off with his paints to the cliffs and seascapes of Cape Breton. He wrote of his month-long exile with joy. "I have not for a long time felt as zestful & ravenous about anything as I did about painting and all that went with it in the heyday of my Nova Scotia wanderings . . . This is what makes life exciting. When you can barely bring yourself to stop at night and are impatient for the next day to start again, wondering what you will meet and produce. I used to feel that way about the lab, but I have not in recent years. I am glad to have found this other side of myself, interested in art and feeling rather than logic and learning."

His landscapes were quick and bold, full of sun and shadow, of near and far. A fan of John Singer Sargent, he believed you should not use more than five basic colors in a single painting. If a picture took more than two hours to paint, it would lose its immediacy, he would say. Sometimes he tinkered with his paintings when he got home but, more often, he would declare the effort "a dud." By that he meant, "Not seen with enough passion, not carefully thought out, with the eye too much on the paper, too little on the thing." When he painted what he considered a failure, Father would often try another picture on the back side of the paper. A wonderful painting done years later of a palm tree on the shores of Lake Como has on its reverse side a very nice view of mountains folding into the lake. This picture, which hung in his bedroom in Paris, has glass on both sides.

"The charm of a watercolor," he once told me, "is the exuberance it gives you, almost like a hallucination. It's so vivid. There it is before you, so real and so compelling. It's a spontaneous response to a spontaneous advance on the part of the world." It's not clear whether he referred then to the art of painting or to the experience of looking at paintings. Later, in the Alaska journal, he described how a painter should feel: "Yesterday, at the lake when we were fishing, the sight of Suzie in her wolf-edged parka with her two boys

Jeffries painting somewhere in Europe in the 1960s.
(Photograph by Olga Lodigensky; collection of the author.)

against the black storm clouds made me look at her with devouring eyes. It must have seemed I was contemplating murder or rape."

A big black-and-white photo taken years later, now in my bathroom, shows Father, totally naked, sitting back-to on a rock in the middle of a stream, painting a picture somewhere in Europe. And the halls and back rooms of the flat in Paris where Father lived at the end of his life were lined with later landscapes he did in France or in Sardinia.

But the Alaska paintings are my favorites—I think because they show people and the intensity of human relationships.

Chapter 13

High Life in Paris

By the time Father left Alaska I am sure he had already decided to quit his frustrating job at Harvard. The university encouraged him; its message was to either stick around or get lost.

At that time the outgoing Truman administration was establishing the brand-new post of science attaché to be launched at U.S. embassies in Paris, London and Tokyo. Possibly Father's tour in Japan had brought him to the attention of the State Department. He was offered the Paris job and accepted with relief. My brother and I, both in our last years at college, were becoming increasingly independent. And, at the age of fifty-one, his own life was half spent. It was time for a change and, like the wild cat on its wild lone, he was off. Once again, Jeff and I had to follow his exploits through long handwritten letters. And now, after the ancient mysteries of Japan and the wildness of Alaska's Brooks Range, the world of the French *haute monde* opened its arms to him.

His initial letter from Paris in February of 1952 was short. He was at a hotel, had been out to dinner with his American aide and had a bottle of Chambertin; the cats yowled all night outside his window but he slept well. A postscript said, typically, "Write soon and don't take all my advice for more than it is worth, which you can only judge for yourself."

Within a week he was invited to a "smart lunch" by Bernard S. Carter, one of the partner-directors of Morgan's Bank in Paris. A butler and maid ushered him into a set of drawing rooms where newly lit fires smoked. Carter's wife hailed from Boston. "I don't know who she was," he wrote, "but she knows many of our friends and relations . . . After dinner I was given an enormous cigar from some that belonged to the old original J. P. Morgan and were marked *Corsair*."

Father was already figuring out French hierarchy: the old Revolutionary nobles, "the Faubourg St. Germain, they call it," versus the later and lesser Napoleonic aristocracy. Carter had arranged for him to live with the Comtesse de Chavignac and her four grown children "in a very nice neighborhood just off the Boulevard des Invalides on the Left Bank . . . I have breakfast in bed or at my writing table and we dine at 7:45 on the dot. It gives me a chance to improve my French. After dinner we talk for a little and then retire to our rooms to get into bed or read. The French have no comfortable chairs to relax in."

By April, again through the offices of Mr. Carter, Father had moved into "really magnificent furnished quarters that are part of a *hôtel particulier* or private mansion belonging to the Comtesse de Leusse and her sister." He described his apartment, just off the fashionable Avenue Foch, in glowing detail. It came with a memorable butler, Marcel, who waited on table in white gloves and kept close track of my father's "doings." Once, in the style of Bertie and Jeeves, my father took Marcel to the de Leusse country house "to show me the way and for an outing. He loves fishing and of course was at once taken into the kitchen and fed." In Paris, Marcel's wife, Marie, in an apron and cap, presided over the ground-floor kitchen and sent elegant meals two floors up to the vast dining room in the dumbwaiter.

And an ancient housekeeper presided over the linens. Father laid in several cases of wine.

Professional life was a whirlwind. His first trip to the French Foreign Office, as America's science attaché, nearly fizzled when the minister rejected some American plan because it came from the embassy's economics section, then seen as hostile to French interests. Father rewrote the memorandum and offered it again from the scientific desk. There were countless American and French scientists to see. He went for a week to England, where he arranged a conference including French scientists to be held that summer. He met a French physiologist who turned out to be the great-great-nephew of the eighteenth-century socialite, Madame Récamier, and was heir to much of her furniture, including the bench on which she was painted by Jacques-Louis David.

Business and pleasure combined as he described in deadpan detail his introduction to the French Academy of Science. "The room was buzzing with old men with white beards, many in morning clothes, shaking hands and gossiping. I must say they were an impressive lot but I felt [the nineteenth-century cartoonist Honoré] Daumier should have been there." He was introduced, then a communication was read "from a little enclosure like a prisoner's dock . . . but nobody paid the slightest attention." There were controversies in the news then about charges of bacterial warfare in World War II and about the execution of Ethel and Julius Rosenberg for selling atomic secrets to Russia. But Father gives these only passing comment.

He paid a formal call on the dean of the Faculty of Science at the Sorbonne, "who is very fat and big like a bear, very shaggy, with hair growing out of his eyes, ears, nose & mouth, it seems, but who speaks like chain lightning. Trying to discuss education with him left

Jeffries in the flat in Paris where he lived while he was U.S. science attaché, about 1952. (Photographer unknown; collection of the author.)

me exhausted at the end of 40 minutes. Fortunately he did 90 percent of the talking. He was very nice. I mean to ask him to dinner one evening soon, when I am *installé* in my new quarters."

Meanwhile, Father wrote, "I manage to see some pictures almost every day [and] by walking everywhere, I manage to get in 6 miles or so every day." He had been taken to the races at Auteuil and given a ticket to a showing at Dior. He met and liked the Princesse de la Tour d'Auvergne, whose ancestry he traced to a Napoleonic general, Prince Berthier de Wagram. He had been to the season's hit play (unnamed) "about a lot of people who become pregnant" and, on his own, to a production of Oedipus Rex presided over by Igor Stravinsky and Jean Cocteau in person.

He entertained and was entertained endlessly. One elegant lunch took place at the Carters' country house near Senlis. Included among the dozen who sat down to table were a rich Mexican mine owner and the New York banker Arthur Sachs. "After lunch," Father wrote, "we all drove off in several cars to the woods to pick daffodils. The Sachses and the Mexican had liveried chauffeurs . . ."

Another time, ignoring Marcel's warning about footpads, he walked through the dark snow-covered Bois de Boulogne to dinner in Neuilly at the home of Julian Allen, also of Morgan's Bank. Among the eighteen guests was the Duchess of Windsor, whom he described as "plain and hard as a rock but [she] carries herself beautifully and moves with a worldly assurance that goes with the international set . . . At table she turns her head right round towards you and looks at you at very close range, really within the focal distance of your eyes." He preferred Lord Ismay, then head of NATO, whom Father saw as "a pleasant old extrovert . . . like an enormously large King Charles spaniel."

Not all of his contacts were with rich Americans and French aristocrats. My father and his aide, Leonard Eyges, went to small laboratories in the countryside; older academicians included him at family dinners and the young Lenormant family took him to the movies and on tablecloth picnics. Will Forbes's sister, Pauline, was in Paris with her husband, Alwin Pappenheimer, who was spending a year at the Institut Pasteur. My mother's first cousin, Libby Metcalf, and her daughter Diana spent a month in his flat. Father pulled a tendon sprinting with Di in the Forest of Fontainbleau.

On his own, Father had a simple routine. He didn't smoke and drank very little. Each day he was up by seven and wrote before breakfast, after which he walked downhill to the embassy. Usually at home by seven at night, he bathed and changed for dinner. Then he would sit in the de Leusse library to read—Balzac, the seventeenth-century letters of Mme de Sévigné or some book on history or travel—and be asleep by eleven. The reading taught him about life and his daily walks cleared his mind. So, when he wrote, he would know what he wanted to say. When we were together, I would watch with amazement as his pencil moved steadily over the pages. Except for occasional inserts, there were few corrections. His spelling was sometimes slapdash but the handwriting was large and clear.

His letters show that he was fascinated by the Paris scene but not entirely sucked in. "My thoughts keep turning towards a more immediate way of life with native peoples," he wrote in April 1952. "All these 'fixings' stand between one and life. To go through life so is like going through a summer day in a cutaway coat, as many good Victorians did. This is a wonderful way of life but really only creates a thirst for the real thing." And a month later, after his lunch at the Carters': "One longs for a more direct contact with life & for the joy & satisfaction of some 'real' achievement like shooting a wolf, or painting a picture, or finishing an experiment."

Did that idea of my father shooting a wolf startle and amuse me when I got his letter, at the age of twenty-two, as it does now? The image that sticks in my mind is a photograph of him as the boy holding a telescope. I could not imagine him with a gun. So, was this just another of his romantic notions?

I went to visit him for a month that summer of 1952 and, following his advice, I brought a hat, white gloves and an evening dress. As it turned out, I hardly needed them. Father wanted to take me with him on a series of visits to outlying laboratories around France. To my dismay, he persuaded Hugh Scott, my Harvard Law School boyfriend, to come with us. Father and the boyfriend became close friends, even sharing a bed in a Brittany farmhouse. I was cut out, and sulked in the back seat of the car while they talked in front. It seemed innocent and inevitable then but, as I grew more furious, the two men became more unapproachable. By the time we had circled the coast and left Avignon the boyfriend had gone. In a way I was glad; I wanted Father to myself.

But he had his own romantic troubles. He had been courting two women in Paris, whom I met that summer. Both were bright and attractive but, he wrote later, one snowy day at her family's country house, he fell out with Monique. "She and I went for a walk in the forest before lunch," he wrote. Then, surprisingly, "I felt somehow antagonistic to her and to the forest, which both seemed so inadequate to that warm, agonizingly beautiful sun . . . I thought of so many wilder landscapes where I could so much better have enjoyed that winter's day." He described feeling "baffled and frustrated." The drive back to Paris in the sunset was the nicest part of the day. Father left his anthropologist friend at her flat and went home "to eat my solitary supper set out by Marcel—a dozen oysters, salad & ham, cheese & fruit, coffee & wine. And now this mood is even stronger & I am glad I have the whole evening ahead of me, alone!"

That evening, I imagine, Father sat in his room at the rue Pergolèse. He'd described it to Will Forbes. "It has lots of pictures of ancestors and old furniture in it. When I have dinner parties I am always made uneasy by the ominous creaking of the Louis XVI chairs. Colbert, an ancestor looks sternly down from the wall." He had been reading poems by James Joyce and wrote one himself:

TO AN AFRICAN MASK

Dark Spirit!
Where did the wood grow;
What the hands, and what the tools
That carved those holes for eyes,
That nose,
The parted lips where
Breath comes hot?

*Hugh Scott, Anne's
boyfriend, and Jeffries
Wyman, on Ile de Bréhat,
in Britanny, 1952.
(Author photo.)*

*Ask not to know such mysteries!
No single hand produced that head;
Only the chips and splinters of
Ten thousand years
Can make a soul.*

*Your hands and mine,
When we take up the gouge and knife,
Are but themselves the tools
Of that old spirit,
Who lived before the ice
And still lives on.*

None of the family was with him. The Metcalf cousins and I had returned to Boston. The lease on the big flat was about to run out and he would move to a smaller place on the Left Bank. He would spend Christmas Day at a big lunch with twenty-four members of the international set. His diplomatic job would go on for more than two years. "I have been drawn to the politics of French science, which are bitter, dirty and most interesting," he wrote in November. Meanwhile he was wondering "where I shall wander in the flesh by and by, when I leave Paris."

Was he content or lonely? Back then, with my own career starting out, I doubt that I worried. Now I think Father, like Rudyard Kipling's vanishing cat, hoped to elude us all—fading, as he so often did, into a kind of "Wet Wild Woods, waving his wild tail and walking by his wild lone."

Soon he would meet Olga Lodigensky and his solitary longings would change. Robert Oppenheimer would reenter his life and affect his career. But that evening, as he digested his oysters, he wrote home: "I have been going to far too many dinners lately & am fed up in every sense. I keep thinking of my eskimos & wishing I were there, eating their meat diet. I wrote Elijah a letter the other day, which someday a plane will drop to him at Anaktuvuk Pass."

Having been banished by Ros, his second wife, Father went to Cape Breton and painted some lovely pictures, including this one (1949). Watercolor. (Collection of the author.)

"Old Sal," a rock formation in Cape Breton, painted by Father in 1949.
Watercolor. (Collection of the author.)

The Kestrel, *aground in the Mussel Ridge Channel, Maine, early 1950s.* Kestrel *was one of only fourteen Fisher's Island sloops, designed and built by the renowned Herreshoff yacht yard. Watercolor. (Collection of the author.)*

The watercolor above,
probably from the 1950s,
depicts Bénéhard, the castle
in France where he visited
Olga Lodigensky, who
would become his third
wife.

Olga in front of a window,
1950s. Watercolor.
(Courtesy of Dimitri de
Faria e Castro.)

Above and at right, two landscapes painted in Europe in the 1950s. Both watercolor. (Courtesy of Dimitri de Faria e Castro.)

A landscape probably done in Italy in the 1950s. Watercolor. (Courtesy of Dimitri de Faria e Castro.)

(Below) In 1951, Father spent a month with a group of Eskimos in Alaska's Brooks Range, in the Arctic Circle. In this painting, Elijah, Father's host, uses a telescope to look for caribou. Watercolor. (Courtesy of Jeffries Wyman, brother of the author.)

Mabel, a Nunamiut girl, playing cat's cradle—also painted during Father's trip to Alaska. Watercolor. (Courtesy of Jeffries Wyman, brother of the author.)

A portrait of Father by his niece, Cicely Aikman, in Paris at age ninety plus. Oil.
(By permission of Cicely Aikman; collection of the author.)

Chapter 14

Olga

My brother and I got our first view of Olga de Faria e Castro in October 1954, roughly a month after Father returned from his embassy job in Paris. The encounter came as a surprise.

We three Wymans were celebrating our first reunion in two and a half years with a week in North Haven and were back at our old routine of sailing, reading and picking mussels for supper. Father had indicated before he left France that he was coming home with bittersweet memories but no ties and no regrets. In his last letter from Paris, on August 31, he wrote, "I do not leave Europe lightly, though I long to find myself at home again . . . I am counting on spending your vacation with you in North Haven or anywhere else. Is there a chance that Jeffy can get the time off?" For Jeff, who was a military policeman with the Army in Boston, and me, newly employed at a Boston publishing company, the sojourn in Maine was a command performance. When Father came home, the Olga of whom he had written seemed to have been left behind.

Not so. We were halfway through the week when the telephone rang and Father announced that Olga had arrived in New York. We were on the island ferry the next morning and back in our flat at the top of Will Forbes's house in Milton that night.

And there she was: a large foreign object in our third-floor Victorian sky parlor, tall and robust with bright blue eyes, high cheekbones and a small mouth that turned down over slightly protruding teeth. By her side, as a sort of duenna, stood a small elderly Russian man. I remember that Father seemed flustered. Olga was torn between laughing and crying. I focused on the elderly man, who told us over an uneasy supper about his recent operation in which a small piece of fetal tissue (human placenta, I gathered) had been inserted under his ribs, and which was supposed to rejuvenate him.

The next morning the small Russian man went off and, as far as I know, we never saw him again. Olga emerged from her assigned room at the back of our third-floor flat and Jeff and I were summoned to attend the unpacking of her large cardboard suitcase.

The contents were a complete jumble of clothes and hard leather shoes, hair-raisingly larded with shards and splinters of some Baccarat crystal wine glasses. Out of the debris, Olga produced presents for us. Jeff has no recollection of this, but I received an Empire fan and a Russian rosary, offerings I accepted like nuclear warheads. That Christmas I unwittingly got my revenge when I gave Olga an embroidered handkerchief and Father a straight razor. Our new stepmother smiled faintly and Father later told me with an embarrassed laugh that she construed my presents as a shroud for herself and a sign that Father should have his throat cut. At the time I thought she was insane; now I think perhaps she was right.

It can't have been easy. Will Forbes was a big fan of Olga's, having met her in Paris, where he succeeded my father as science attaché, but my mother's family of Cabots, Forbeses and Paines was baffled and amused when Father's Russian lady was taken around for a viewing. Jeff, as I recall, took no stance. But I was outraged at being caught once more in the middle of a relationship I loathed. I was so angry that one night, after I'd roused Olga for a late telephone call, I went and lay down like a wolfhound on the threshold of my father's room to prevent her from coming in. Father just laughed and went back to sleep.

But he was feeling trapped. He privately consulted my mother's sister Susan in Cambridge and, when Olga became so tense that she lost her voice for three days, he sent her to talk to Aunt Susan too. Aunt Susan later recalled Father's "urgent desire to flee," and told me she'd advised them to see "a family specialist." Instead, I came home from work one June day in 1955 and learned that Father and Olga had been married that afternoon at a registry office in Quincy. Their marriage lasted for thirty-five years and was a surprising success.

I can't believe I hadn't seen it coming. I find now that Father's first mention of her was on January 20, 1953. Then, still in Paris, he had moved to the Left Bank at the start of the year and had written, "This evening my Russian friend Olga de Castro is coming to dinner. Her husband was one of the large landowners of Lithuania and she tells me of the Feudal life she used to live there before the war when Lithuania was an independent country—riding every morning before breakfast, living in a 13th Century castle with 62 rooms, accessible only by horse in winter. Her father [once chief of staff of the Tsar's armed forces] was the last Imperial governor of the Crimea and still lives, as an old man, in Paris and dreams of someday going back to Russia, which of course he never will. She knows many of the characters in *War and Peace.*"

Despite its fairytale flavor, this sounded like many other of his casual encounters, sandwiched between accounts of his "doings"—everyone had a cold or the grippe; an American friend was coming to Paris to see him.

A few weeks later he and Olga had a rendezvous at the Russian Orthodox Church on the rue Daru. Father had been there quite a while and was admiring a Byzantine fresco of Christ when, he wrote later, "A tall slim figure in black, carrying a candle, walked resolutely past me, threaded her way through the worshippers, proceeded up to the little altar in front of an icon, fixed her candle there, kissed the icon and kneeled to pray for some time, hidden by a kind of screen. It was Olga but we did not speak until the end."

How Father must have loved the melodrama. And how he must have been intrigued when Olga told him that her marriage, to a distant cousin when she was nineteen, had taken place against her will. For months, she had locked herself in her room at Rodony Castle every night, leaving the new husband outside. At one point, she even ran off for several days with a band of gypsies who had been camping near the castle. Olga's marriage to the Russo-Portuguese Nicolas de Faria lasted twelve years, but they were estranged after the birth of their son, Dimitri, in 1939.

Now, responding to Father's interests, Olga took him on a Sunday visit to an aged Russian scientist, whom he discovered to be "none other than Winogradsky, the founder, really, of soil bacteriology." They found the ninety-four-year-old dying of gangrenous feet in a nearly deserted outpost of the Institut Pasteur, attended by a niece and a daughter. The scene, which Father described in gloomy but breathless detail, was "nostalgic and tragic." Yet there is no indication that Father, with his diplomatic connections, nor Olga, with her network of Russians, took any steps to ease the old Winogradsky's last days.

Meanwhile, Father's life as science attaché had evidently continued with meetings, dinner parties and off-duty visits to art museums. He still saw his friend, Françoise Hageneau, whom I'd met and liked in 1952. But by the spring of 1953, he was taking Olga on long Sunday walks in the royal forests around Paris, then bringing her

Bénéhard, in the Loire Valley in France, where Father spent time in the early 1950s visiting Olga, soon to be his third wife. Photo is from around 1953. (Photographer unknown.)

back to eat supper, seated on the floor "Japanese style," and to read aloud from *War and Peace*. In return she invited him that May to visit Bénéhard, a cousin's chateau on the Loire River where, from June to October, Olga was hostess to as many as fifteen Russian relatives and their children.

His first visit sounds like a scene from Cocteau's movie *Orpheus*. Arriving in the pitch dark on that rain-swept Friday, Father wrote that he found himself

> in a big hall with a stone-flagged floor of limestone and black marble, with a heavy stone staircase leading up from it, the turning steps worn hollow.
>
> There were oil lamps in various strategic places but it was all very dark and the shadows had the best of it. Far away at the end of some passage I heard Olga's voice in answer to my call and made

my way to it. At the end of a long room a door opened into another room where there was an immense fire, a table set for two and Olga waiting. There were lots of apple blossoms and flowers and a most curious little coffee pot with an oil flame under it, showing light through the translucent walls of the white porcelain stand.

It all gave me a wonderful sense of arrival. And then to be taken on a tour through the confusing expanse of rooms, including a huge kitchen with its long table and fireplace—all by lamplight! I felt I was in [a novel by Sir] Walter Scott with all the portraits looking down on me. There was a hot water bottle in the bed in my panelled room and more apple blossoms on the mantelpiece.

Jeff and I never saw Bénéhard except in Father's watercolors, painted on successive weekends at the chateau. These pictures are of romantic turrets with open windows and long walls of yellow stone. But it seems significant to me now that there are no people in them and no mention of other inhabitants in his letters, though we met several of the guests later on and Bénéhard was a frequent subject of conversation.

To me now there is something creepy about that, as there is in my father's account of his second day on the premises. "I woke up to a most glorious day," he wrote, "and to the sound of chickens, ducks, distant cocks, the crunching of cart wheels and the lowing of cows. It is curious to see a place by daylight after an arrival at night—and such an arrival as that. It is like the denouement of a detective story."

Then, without pause, his letter continued. "The chateau is not well kept up. The court is full of weeds; grass is growing between the stone steps and, in the big tower at the end of the court, the ceiling and floor crashed down [during a mudslide] several years ago and killed the guardian and his family." Father's reaction to the tragedy here was the same as his response to old Winogradsky, minutely observant but totally disengaged. It is as though he were looking through a microscope, seeing a painting or reading a book.

Olga herself sounds phantasmagorical. One weekend a caravan of gypsies camped near Bénéhard. Recalling perhaps her earlier escapade at Rodony, Olga led the household to their site, hoping the group would dance and sing. When nothing happened, she took the gypsies off "at a run" to a bistro to ply them with wine but, Father reported, the gypsies still refused to perform. Another time, Father wrote, she stopped at a nearby farmhouse and bought ten dozen eggs, to be delivered to the chateau, to take back to Paris. Looking back, I wonder if these were echoes from Lithuania or the haunting from real hunger during World War II.

Stranger still was the fact that, during their two-year courtship, there was little contact between Father and Olga's thirteen-year-old son. Dimitri must have simply seemed to be just one of the children around the place, specially loved by his grandparents and Olga's sister, Marina. When I met Dimitri for the first time, eleven years later, he told me that he had felt outside the relationship until after Father and Olga were married. Given Father's unwillingness to have children with Ros, perhaps Olga was taking no chances.

It didn't occur to me then that deserting their children presented a common bond. Putting children second may have been an accepted practice in their crowd. More important to me was Olga's focus on marriage as the only natural status for women and her determination to play any role that would please and interest the intellectual, artistic and ephemeral man who had come into her life. She did love my father; she knew how to please him; and she took great care of him for the rest of her life. I watched from an increasing distance, at first angry, then dutiful, but finally accepting and even grateful toward her.

Olga loved gossip and melodrama and attracted people in trouble. But I distrusted her confidences and, at the age of twenty-four, found her advice infuriating, condescending and absurd. And she never let up. In October 1961, early in my career as a reporter at the *Boston Globe*, she wrote, "You should not feel married to your work. If you cannot bring yourself to marry anyone, do at least get out of your almost masculine work . . . I know how difficult it is for you to find somebody on the same level with you. But if you don't learn from that, you may as well get in love with somebody successful in another field without being an intellectual . . ." In another letter, four years later, she urged, "You are so big and it is difficult to find a partner. Try to become smaller and there may be someone."

And, in August of 1968, when I had just bought my own house in Cambridge, she wrote to congratulate me. But then she went on: "There are so many lost dogs on this earth that maybe you will one day open your door to one of them. He will remain faithful and with time become a faithful guardian of you and your home." In a postscript she added, "Don't misunderstand. What I mean by a lost dog is a cozy, helpful and devoted human being."

The idea that I should give up my masculine job, that I should suppress my intellectual personality, that I should marry a successful if boring man who would attend to me like a dog—all this seemed to me insulting and out of touch.

Furthermore, Father, true to himself as always, had failed to alert us or to understand how Jeff and I might feel. He was, perhaps, ambivalent himself. Back in June of 1953 he had written of Olga, "You need not think I have plans for marrying her or anyone else. Perhaps it is my great weakness that I don't seem ready to give myself to anybody or anything unconditionally . . ." Nine months later, with his embassy job closing down, he was thinking of moving back to Brookline by himself. "Olga gets very moody and depressed at the idea of my going away," he wrote. "I don't blame her and I feel very badly." Then he added in very large handwriting, "I seem to prefer the world of experiences to the companionship of any one person . . ."

As the date for his departure from Paris approached, he wrote, "This languorous June twilight makes me think of the old days in Brookline before the deluge of changes, when your mother and I used to have supper outdoors on the little folding table I made. And afterwards stroll across the lawn, sometimes onto the terrace and the knoll beyond at Grandma's. I can almost smell the wisteria now. And, after dark, the fireflies. You and Jeffy were upstairs, sometimes turning uneasily, occasionally calling, but more often dead to everything and limp as rags." He had often expressed a desire to find a little house in the country near Boston where Jeff and I would join him, as in old times. But this unrealistic vision had come too late.

Jobless and homeless, it was now my father's turn to be cast away. After their marriage he and Olga remained in Milton for a few awkward weeks; then she returned to France on her own. That summer he was once more in North Haven, planning a cruise with Jeff and his school friend Bebo Porter. He apologized in a letter for making "the last two weeks overwhelming" with Olga's departure. Then he recalled "the first day of 26 years ago when your mother brought me here, to birds, woods, seclusion and a peace which has been much altered, not only here but everywhere."

But the marriage lasted and, once again, a job turned up. By November 1955 Father and Olga were en route to Cairo, where he had a job as head of the Middle East bureau of UNESCO, the United Nations Educational, Scientific and Cultural Organization. From then on, he would come back to visit us, and we sometimes went to see him abroad. But his marriage to Olga marked the belated end of our childhood connection to him.

Chapter 15

Egypt

When I visited Father in Egypt he had been in Cairo as director of UNESCO's Middle East Science Cooperation Office for over a year and had been out sculling on the Nile when British jets strafed the river during the Suez Crisis of 1956. I flew in overnight from London where I was working for Chatto & Windus, an English publishing company. I had agreed to wait at the airport, but Father and his Egyptian driver were there to meet me when my plane landed at 3:20 A.M. on May 2, 1957.

The long drive through the breaking dawn took us along streets lined with palm trees and donkey carts heading for town. Father and Olga had been in the flat since April and he had written that it was "a penthouse with wonderful [outdoor] terraces on the 10th floor of a big new apartment house. We have half of the top floor. It is in Gizeh and in front it has a full panorama of the Nile with the sight of all the triangular-sailed feluccas passing up & down." Olga greeted me with a cup of tea and I went to sleep to the roaring of lions from the zoo behind the house. If I stood on the little balcony outside my room, I could almost see the pyramids lit by the sunrise.

My father entertained me royally during my month's stay. The UNESCO office, somewhere behind the old Shepheard's Hotel, on the east side of the river, did not seem to keep him very busy. He would come back to the penthouse for lunch and often brought two of his young assistants with him. One was Chaffik Shamas, a cuddly Egyptian man who had been to an English school in Cairo. The other was a tall, thin Spaniard named Francisco Bennet who was preoccupied with a plan to kidnap his year-old son from the wife who had divorced him and returned to her family in Lebanon.

Francisco was furnishing an apartment for the boy and, while Father returned to work in the afternoon, Francisco would take me to the old bazaar, called the Muski, to look for ancient wooden screens with open-work and carved panels—items commonly used to protect Egyptian women on their balconies from unseemly glances by passers-by. We would wander through the clamorous alleys into dusty workshops where mint tea was always brought while business was discussed. Sometimes, after supper, all five of us, including Father, Olga and Chaffik, would go to the bazaar together. The Muski was even busier at that hour. I remember watching a man flip circles of sweet dough into huge thin pancakes that were baked and folded and brought to us with the mint tea, while Father bargained on my behalf for bubbly hand-blown bowls and goblets like the ones he and Olga already had.

One night Chaffik took us all to see a famous belly dancer who performed in a big embroidered tent somewhere near the pyramids. One morning we got up before dawn and galloped on beautiful spirited horses across the desert from Gizeh to the much older step-pyramid at Sakkara, where Olga and Father's driver, Hafiz, met us with coffee and melons. One of the tombs, half buried in sand, contained twenty-five black granite sarcophagi which, according to Chaffik, had housed mummified Apis bulls sacred to Ptah, the god of Memphis.

There was so much going on that it is hard to remember it all. After twelve months in Cairo, Olga had decided to build a windbreak and pergola on the big roof terrace. Mokhtar, our house servant, would stand on the terrace in his turban and long white robe, urging the workers on and translating Olga's instructions. He came from the Sudan, had ceremonial scars on both cheeks, and decorated the lunch table with flowering artichokes. Hafiz drove me everywhere and taught me to count to ten in Arabic. His English was sketchy and he once surprised Father by telling him, "Madame is an angle," meaning of course that she was an angel.

There were lunch parties with Europeans living on houseboats at Zamalek, an island in the Nile. We were invited to a special exhibition of tent-pegging and dressage with Arab stallions at a desert arena outside the city. We spent an afternoon at a little village where the clay houses piled up like beehives. We went to a Cairo hospital, Dar El-Shefa, to see an old Egyptian acquaintance who talked nonstop while a barber shaved him with a straight razor. We visited the National Museum and took a moonlit drive through the vast spooky Mamluk cemetery on the Mokattam Hills. I rowed with Father and went water-skiing with some young Egyptians on the Nile.

Sometimes on weekends, Father, Olga and I would drive north to the new but still-deserted Mediterranean resort of Ras Al-Bar, where the houses reminded me of the shacks on the dunes of Cape Cod. From there we took a felucca upriver to a fruit plantation for lunch with Egyptian friends. Once, we made the long desert drive from Cairo to Suez with Father's closest friend, Judge Jasper Brinton, an elderly Philadelphian who represented the local office of the International Court. The judge took us for an overnight cruise on his small sailboat, twenty-eight miles down the Gulf of Suez to Ain Sukhna, where we anchored against a wild backdrop of hills, swam in the hot spring, weathered a windy night and, in the morning, snorkeled over bright fish and huge bear-paw clams.

*Olga and her dachshund
Strega in Egypt, en route
to a picnic lunch, 1957.
(Author photo.)*

Another time, I was sent off alone with Olga by train to Karnak and Luxor. Without my father to push me, I ignored Luxor and walked alone to Karnak's Temple of Amun with its alley of ram-headed sphinxes, its roofless hall of papyrus-shaped columns and the wonderful wall of hieroglyphs depicting the conquests of Thutmosis III. Olga stayed behind to gossip with the manager of the Mina Palace Hotel. In the wake of the Suez affair, there were no other tourists in town. The next day we crossed the river to see the underground tombs in the Valley of the Kings and our guide advised me to buy a fake tomb-chipping, saying, "After all, it was made by descendants of the original artisans."

Toward the end of my visit, Father and I drove to Alexandria and stayed two nights at a flowery little English pensione. We walked along the Corniche and drove east to the beach at Abu Qir, where the English Lord Nelson sank Napoleon's French fleet in 1798. Nothing remained but a ruined lighthouse, some fishermen drying their nets under the palms, and perhaps ghosts. The next day we drove west along the coast toward the site of the huge World War II battle at El Alamein and were almost arrested by a coastguardsman on a camel who encountered us taking an impromptu swim in the sea. On the way home, we left the car and walked over the desert to the old Coptic monastery at Wadi Natrun, where one of the few remaining monks gave us tea and told us to watch out for horned vipers as we returned to the car. We saw none, only their twisty tracks on the sand.

For me, at the age of twenty-seven, the month's visit was easy and fun. When I left on May 28 I flew back to a successful job and a nice English boyfriend in London. I'd had a marvelous year and the trip to Egypt capped it off. I didn't love Olga but I had come to understand her better. She had not tried to remake me or my life, at least on this visit. She would sit quietly knitting or puttering about with Mokhtar while Father and I read aloud after supper, as we had done since I was a child. She had fostered my entourage of Chaffik, Francisco and my father's young Greek secretary, Ica, and I was interested in her elaborate plans for a bamboo shack on the terrace rooftop. Still, I was angry and jealous when I woke up one night while we were cruising the Gulf of Suez aboard Judge Brinton's boat to find that Father, who had started out sleeping near me on the rolling deck, had gone below and was cuddled with her in a berth.

And, at fifty-six, my father, who had just discovered the Middle East for himself, had been clearly delighted to show me around. The day I flew north back to England he wrote me a letter. "Dearest Anne," it began.

> You are speeding away over the shores of Greece and I have just finished breakfast. Olga is fast asleep and Mokhtar has gone off to do errands. What an empty house you have left behind!
>
> ... I am glad this is Sunday & that I can catch my breath & balance. It is the first weekend we have not been off somewhere & going hard since you came ... Now I want to savor your visit. I look forward to lying in the long chair—i.e., the chair with the footrest—reading *The Moonstone* & letting my mind wander and perhaps go rowing & having tea in the pergola & not seeing anyone. That is the way I feel ... I am not really homesick but your coming & going has turned my mind towards home. Someday I must come back to that world. But in the meantime there are so many things that beckon—the Dinkas!

It is a peculiar mixture of reflection and excitement. He's enjoying being alone but thinks of new social contacts. He writes of lying in the long chair, then thinks of going out sculling on the Nile. He ponders returning to Boston and Brookline and all the old family things, then immediately conjures up plans for a trip to visit the Dinka people in the southern Sudan, who, he wrote in a subsequent letter to Jeff, are "among the least changed and least civilized in Africa, they say."

Rereading the letter several years after his death, it seems absolutely typical. It harks back to his years at Naushon when he would spend hours alone with a book in front of the fire, then describe paddling through current and storm to Woods Hole. It is like his times in Japan, contemplating art and religions, then hiking over steep remote peninsulas to hail a fisherman who could get him back to his bus or train. It echoes his years in Paris, first enthralled by encounters with the rich and famous, then withdrawing to the countryside to paint and eat kitchen suppers. It even goes back to Father's college years, when he stayed up talking about "Nomograms" with Professor L.J. Henderson and John Edsall, then went home to Wellesley for tea and reading aloud with his mother.

It makes me feel calm and somehow grown up to think of this now. And perhaps my visit to Egypt did mark a first shift in our relationship, where I seem to have had my adult feet on the ground while my father was still flitting about in the air.

Father and Olga stayed in Cairo for another year. His UNESCO jurisdiction stretched from Casablanca to New Delhi and, while based in Cairo, Father had managed again to go off on his "wild lone." Once on a trip to Morocco, he took off for a week's "walk" in the Atlas Mountains, armed with only a sandwich and a sweater. And I have inherited two larger-than-life wooden tomb figures that he brought back from the Hindu Kush on the remote borders of Afghanistan. There was an interlude in June 1957 when Olga visited Paris, and another early in 1958 when they both came to Boston for a month's stay. By the end of March they were back in Cairo, planning a weekend stay at the Kahils' plantation on the Nile Delta. But the UNESCO job had only three months to go, and by June 30, 1958, Olga had returned to France, and Jeff and Father were on a plane to Juba on the White Nile in the southern Sudan.

⋯

For the next thirty-six days my father and brother trekked through Equatorial Africa, drinking blood and milk with the Dinkas, eating honey and antelope with the Pygmies, slogging through heat and rain, waiting for strayed porters, hitching rides with infrequent trucks, and, finally, winding up opposite Edward Stanley's ominously named "Camp de la Faim," below Murchison Falls, where my father suffered from an infected ankle and had an attack of malaria.

It was a very hard trip and not always a happy one. Jeff was embarrassed to be larking around in the outback with half-starved porters who carried their tent, food and belongings. And Father told me later that days went by when Jeff didn't speak to him.

At my father's memorial service in Cambridge, Massachusetts, thirty-seven years later, Jeff made it sound funny. "One time Father wanted to go into another part of the country and asked the local official about getting there," he told us. "The District Commissioner was shocked and said we would have to cross a vast swamp where we would be eaten by all kinds of bugs and perhaps crocodiles. All the people who lived on the far side were hostile." Jeff paused. "I knew this was just the wrong thing to say to my father," he continued. "It just egged him on. The next day we set out, crossed the swamp, and were not eaten up. And when we got to the other side, the people were extremely friendly." Everyone at the service laughed.

But that was the last such trip my father and brother took together.

They parted in Africa and flew home separately. Jeff came back to Boston via Belgium, and Father flew to Paris via Tripoli and Nice, where his plane lost an engine. When Father landed in France he learned that Olga's mother had died of cancer the day before.

Again, his reaction was characteristic. Father reported that he found Olga and her family "all in great grief, naturally. The thin wasted body, the features sharpened by suffering, was laid out and a nun was reading beside it," he wrote at the close of his trip diary. Then, without a break, he went on: "That afternoon I went off by myself, wandering across the Pont Alexandra III and down into the Tuileries. It was a phenomenally hot day—the hottest on record—and there was a wonderful sense of abandon about everything—mothers, nurses, children, amorous couples sitting or strolling under the shade of the big trees. What a change from Africa. It was the world of Renoir."

Chapter 16

Adrift

My father's life seemed to swing between melodrama and suspenseful calm. But he was fearless in the face of both. Before packing up for the Sudan and his departure from Egypt, he had written on May 6, 1958, "I have been asked to go to Japan as Science Advisor and expect to do so after Jeff and I finish our African wanderings." Seventeen days later another letter said, "It seems quite definite now that I shall go to Japan. Only such formalities as clearance remain." But the clearance never came.

The agent of his disappointment, he always believed, was the aftermath of the so-called "Army-McCarthy hearings" of 1954, which produced a climate of fear in the United States, not unlike that after the 9/11 attacks on New York and Washington in 2001.

Late in 1953 J. Robert Oppenheimer, his old friend from Harvard and Cambridge, England, had visited Father in Paris and, in the course of other conversation, had asked if Father would help the American-born leftist Haakon Chevalier obtain the renewal of his U.S. passport. Father had invited Chevalier to lunch but apparently done nothing more. Oppenheimer, who had resigned from Los Alamos in October 1945, would lose his security clearance on May 27,

1954, on grounds that he had past Communist ties and, as chairman of the Atomic Energy Commission's General Advisory Committee, he had publicly opposed development of the hydrogen bomb as a weapon of "genocide."

My father himself had been interviewed that spring of 1954 during a visit to Rome in his role as science attaché at the U.S. Embassy in Paris. His description of the episode, in a letter he wrote at the time, reflected his refusal to be cowed or to feel his diplomatic career was in danger. The encounter read like something out of a John le Carré novel.

He wrote that he had spent the day trying in vain to negotiate U.S. visas for some European scientists and had come back to his pensione to find a message from a Mr. Brown at the American Embassy in Rome. The message said that a Mr. Winter, from the legal attaché's office in Paris, was flying in that night to talk to him. At half past midnight Mr. Brown arrived at my father's rooms to say that Mr. Winter had missed the plane but would arrive in the morning. "So," he wrote, "I promised to see him after my nine o'clock appointment with the Consul General and went back to sleep."

Right off, he surmised that the interview might revolve around Oppenheimer, and his letter continued, "At the appointed hour, we met in Mr. Brown's office. Both men flashed things—F.B.I. cards—at me and I felt for a moment like a spy. It soon turned out, however, that my suspicion was correct and we spent the whole morning going over the most minute details of everything I knew of Oppenheimer. This resulted in a long memorandum of four or five pages for me to sign. I had been invited to a lunch party by the director of the Italian Institute of Hygiene, to which I felt bound to go, and so they sent me off to keep my appointment in an embassy car. But I promised to come back right afterwards to sign the statement, when it should be typed. Winter would then fly it back to Paris, whence it would be cabled to Washington.

"It seemed to me a little ludicrous, but I couldn't help regarding it as ominous too, like the whole inquiry . . . Incidentally, I am told that my testimony did Oppenheimer a real service. I only hope so," he wrote, and then he inserted, "though it seems ridiculous."

Of course it was not ridiculous in those scary days of red-baiting, blacklisting and political upheaval. Joseph McCarthy's dem-agoguery was censured by the U.S. Senate later in 1954 and McCarthy died in 1957. Robert Oppenheimer remained the director of the Institute for Advanced Studies at Princeton University and, in 1963, was personally awarded the Atomic Energy Commission's Enrico Fermi Award by President Lyndon Johnson in the White House. But, though Father occasionally attributed the denial of his clearance for the Japan posting to his having a Russian wife and an indiscreet French cook, he really believed it was his support of Oppenheimer that ended his diplomatic career.

On his return from Egypt, Father was still hopeful that he might win a posting to Japan. On February 4, 1959, he wrote, "Would you please have a look at our mail in Milton and, if there is anything of interest, be sure to forward it." When nothing came, he must have considered the case closed. He had no concrete plan for the next stage of his life. For the ensuing nine months, he and Olga led a gypsy life, wandering around Europe, visiting Russian connections of hers. Olga did not like America and Father was already becoming the expatriate that he would be from now on. Together they were looking for a place to settle, and wondering, at Father's age of fifty-eight, what he might do. He wrote lots of letters describing visits to spooky German castles, Italian hill towns and the Greek monasteries of Mount Athos.

On May 22 he wrote from Athens,

I have been thinking of coming back to the U.S.A, in June or July and finding a real place to live . . . and also looking for something that I should like to do. But, since that would probably be something abroad, I am not sure whether it would not be foolish to acquire cares and responsibilities at present. I am thinking at the moment of finding a *pied-à-terre* in the south of France, perhaps near Aix en Provence, which would be inexpensive and where I could put all our household things from Egypt, which are stored in Marseilles.

   If I wanted to make one or two long journeys on my own, Olga would probably feel more at home here than in the U.S.A. On the other hand, if I took a job somewhere in Europe or elsewhere in some form of government overseas activity, it would be handy or, if not, I could give it up . . . Eventually, of course, I do mean to come home to live. If you have any thoughts about all of this, let me know; but don't concern yourself with what, after all, are my problems. If I do stay on this side of the water this summer, would you conceivably want to come over to join us?

His uncertainty was not new, nor was his request for our "thoughts" from home. But both seemed more acute than usual for him. And clearly Olga's wishes were a new and powerful factor in the ultimate decision.

On July 4, then back in Paris, he wrote to Jeff,

My plans are not yet settled though I suppose I shall come home for a while in the autumn . . . I do wish we could have another trip together [like the one to the Sudan]. Sometime perhaps we can before I get too old and you get tied down by work and family . . . I think often of the glorious autumns in the New England countryside and of the long walks one can take there, as Anne and I did last autumn. I think too of Penobscot Bay and the Cape. Certainly I have no idea of spending all the rest of my days in Europe but still, as a headquarters in these coming years, it has something to offer. I am wondering, too, where you will be living—you and Anne—for I should like it to be possible to get together often. If ever I shall become a grandfather [a vain hope, partly driven by his own misgivings about matrimony and children] I should like to be a practising one and not a mere name on the other side of the earth.

He also wrote another poem, an echo of his mood:

It is not always fortune to be straight and tall
Passing unheeding through the world.
Some things only the frail can see and do;
Some things only the bent and bruised can understand,
Like broken beach grass
Drawing circles in the sand.

On their way back to Paris from Greece, he and Olga had seen a house north of Dijon. Father thought of buying the place with money inherited from my mother and Grandma Cabot and increased by shrewd management in Boston.

"It is a house built about ninety or a hundred years ago by a marshal of France who was tutor to the sons of Napoleon III," he wrote. "It is in a nice region, not far from a lake, with a park of three or four acres completely surrounded by a wall and with fine trees in it. There is a nice *potager* with a fine bed of strawberries. There is a cottage where a couple live, a barn with a cow and a garage with living quarters above . . . I must decide what the rest of my life is to be and act accordingly. I do wish you were here to talk it over with me. Olga wants to live somewhere where she can have the house full of people. I flinch, unreasonably perhaps, at the idea of the U.S.A."

Given Father's loathing of American materialism and his longing for places like the Arctic and the Sudan, his misgivings about the U.S.A. seem inevitable. Instead of the Dijon house, though, he and Olga rented a small house in the Savoy for the summer. "No, I have nothing in my mind in the way of a job," he wrote on July 11, 1959, "but I am inclined to go to Washington next autumn to see how things look. I rather doubt whether I should like the mixture of country life in France and intervals of distant travel without anything more demanding; but I am at least going to spend the summer here . . . Olga wants, more than anything, to be able to make a home somewhere—do the cooking, provide coziness and have people about her. I find my mind already dwelling on far places in Africa, Asia and the Arctic . . ."

By October 8, he wrote that he was "getting restless and bored . . . When I came it was very hot and the days were very long—the long early days of July in Europe. Now it is dusk when we get in from an afternoon walk and [in the morning] the sun does not show above the Grand Colombier until after seven. We have a fire every morning and evening in the big Savoyard fireplace in the kitchen where a man can stand upright. After lunch it is good to sit in the sun on the sheltered stone steps, which lead down from the terrace to the field, and store up the heat of midday. The chestnuts are falling fast and with them the big brown leaves. The vines have been stripped of their grapes and are losing their green too. In the evening the blue smoke hangs over the village like a sheet and behind, in the background, rise the big hills. We have been through the *vendange* and everything smells of wine—I feel I never want to drink again. It is all very beautiful but still, as I say, I am getting restless."

Rescue was on its way. James D. Watson, a Harvard tutee of my father's and co-discoverer at Cambridge University in 1953 of the double helix structure of DNA, had been to visit them at "Clos des Vignes." Another visitor was John Kendrew, also of Cambridge University, who was working on the structure of myoglobin. Kendrew invited Father to spend a month to six weeks at Cambridge and arranged for him to take the rooms of Richard Keynes, a nephew of the economist Maynard Keynes, at Peterhouse College while my father worked to complete his chapter on hemoglobin for the never-published Volume Two of his book with John Edsall on biochemistry.

Preparing for his move across the English Channel, Father traveled to Switzerland and rented a small apartment in Lausanne for Olga and her son, Dimitri, who would be studying there for his baccalaureate exams in March. Lausanne was full of Russians, Father wrote, and "the lake sports many white swans who cruise along the shore and add greatly to the prospect—horrid things really, snarling and hissing, combining the worst of the birds and the snakes."

By October 26 my father was at Peterhouse, dining at high table with the Archbishop of Canterbury, another dinner guest. "He is a teetotaler, which seems a pity for one who has had so many opportunities," Father wrote. His rooms over the archway joining the chapel to the north side of the college had no bathroom, "but my gyp, one of the last [male college servants] of Cambridge, whose name is Goose (!), brings me hot water when he wakes me up at 7:30 every morning and tells me the time and state of the weather." Peterhouse was the oldest of the university colleges and reputed to have the best food.

But more exciting than these aspects of what Father called "the monastic life" was the beehive of scientific activity that surrounded him. The person he saw most was Kendrew. "His work on myoglobin is coming to fine fruition and matches that of Max Perutz on hemoglobin," Father wrote on December 1. "I should think they will get the Nobel Prize in a couple of years when it is more complete and I believe it will mark the beginning of a new era in the study of proteins.

"By back-breaking analysis of a vastly complicated set of data obtained by X-ray diffraction, they have been able to work out the structure of these two molecules, one of which is really a tetrameter [having four sub-units] of the other, as some of us suspected but hardly dared to believe. Kendrew, whose work has gone farther because myoglobin is only one-quarter as complicated as hemoglobin, is making a huge model of it in which he has employed over five miles of steel rod to support the elements that represent the atoms, or rather chains of atoms. It shows for the first time the existence of helices in a real protein—long spiral chains of amino acids, about three and a half of them to a turn. It will also show how these chains bend and fold to make the solid globular molecule, but that is not yet clear. All the helices," he noted, "seem to be right-handed."

Kendrew and Perutz did win the Nobel Prize in chemistry in 1962. The same year the prize in physiology and medicine went to Watson, Francis Crick and London University's Maurice Wilkins, while the Peace Prize went to Linus Pauling of Cal Tech, in Pasadena, for his promotion of a ban on atomic testing in the atmosphere. Pauling had already won the prize in chemistry in 1954 "for his work on the nature of the chemical bond and its elucidation of the structure of complex substances"—another seminal finding that had an impact on my father's research on binding and linkage in the function of macromolecules like hemoglobin.

⁕

I have quoted from Father's letters at length because I'm in awe of his resilience and fearlessness in the face of uncertainty. I'd been through a similar period myself.

I got back from England in the spring of 1957 to find that my place at Houghton Mifflin had been filled. Unfazed at the time, I took off on an eight-week camping trip around the United States with a friend from Chatto & Windus, the publishing house in London where I had worked the previous year. That fall I found what might be called a handyman job with two men who were starting a publishing business in New York City. I shared a flat in Greenwich Village with an old college friend, but after only five months took off in February 1958 to fly a small Cessna across a wintry countryside to California with my older chum Wendy Howell, the daughter of William Thompson, one of the defense lawyers for Sacco and Vanzetti.

That summer I abandoned the New York job for good and moved to an apartment on San Francisco's Russian Hill. Wendy and I took summer courses at Berkeley and cruised the Sacramento River in her houseboat, the *Squarehead*. I got engaged to an old friend from Brookline, who was flying jet fighters for the Air Force at San Rafael. Wendy gave a party for us in September but, among my friends and Wendy's, my fiancé seemed dull. We fought on the way to his flat in Sausalito and the next morning I broke off the engagement and was on my way back to Boston, still single and free and with no idea what the future would hold.

Olga wanted me to be heartbroken. But Father's only reaction was to ask in a letter from Paris, "What happened to Pete?" and to recall our trip around France with Hugh Scott. "I wonder if I should have given you more encouragement in marrying [Hugh] but I suspect, if you had married him, it would have ended badly," adding unhelpfully, "though one cannot be sure." Years later, I got a surprise call from my ex-fiancé, en route to his son's boarding school. Over the phone, Pete updated me about his own life for some forty-five minutes but never asked about mine. I was glad I had got away.

But it is one thing to chase the stars in one's twenties; it is quite another to be cut off in mid-career and on a foreign continent when, like my father, you are in your late fifties. He had been away from Harvard and scientific research for a decade, was considering turning from science to art, and had entered a new way of life with Olga. But, in fact, Father had kept in close touch with scientists in his field. Now that field was exploding with new discoveries and new understanding and he was ready to go back to work.

By October of 1959 I was sharing a flat with a friend in Harvard Square and had obtained a job at the *Boston Globe*, work that would hold me for thirty-one years. Jeff, who had ended his own wanderings, was getting a master's degree in math at Boston University and living nearby.

Father, meanwhile, had been offered a research job at Cambridge. He and John Kendrew were involved with others in planning a European Molecular Biology Organization to be based in Heidelberg. Also, one day at lunch with Jeffrey Roughton at Trinity College, Father had been introduced to the Italian scientist Eraldo Antonini, who had talked of the research on hemoglobin being done by his boss, Alessandro Rossi-Fanelli at the big cancer institute, Regina Elena, in Rome.

Early in 1960, Father went to visit the Italian lab for a month, and in May he agreed to join the group for a year. That year would turn into twenty-five years. Once again, Father had landed, cat-like, on his feet. On the surface, at least, it seemed we were all three settling down.

Chapter 17

Science

Father and Olga moved to Rome in September 1961, where he quickly reentered the scientific world he had left behind in 1952 when he resigned from Harvard to join the embassy in Paris.

Today, taking even six months off can put a researcher hopelessly behind. But life was different in the early 1960s. Eraldo Antonini and his colleagues admired my father's earlier work, particularly the theoretical articles he had written in 1937 and 1951 on the way macromolecules might function, and they invited him to join their group even though he had been away from research for nearly a decade.

An additional attraction may have been the fact that my father would not need the usual suite of rooms stuffed with expensive equipment and buzzing with graduate students, because his primary workplace was in his head. His greatest insights, he often said, came on the long walks he took in the countryside. And I can see him now, seated in a small armchair after breakfast, his back to the light, with a lined legal pad on his knee and a yellow pencil in his hand, putting his thoughts and theorems down on paper.

He rarely talked about his work to me, but I gathered that his role at Regina Elena was, to oversimplify it, dreaming up models or equations expressed in formal mathematical terms to describe the binding patterns of large and complex molecules. His approach was far removed from the world of the laboratory. All around him, others, including Antonini and younger scientists like Maurizio Brunori and Emilia Chiancone, were making measurements of hemoglobin under various experimental conditions. Working with a small number of postdoctoral fellows from the United States, they generated mounds of data. Father's role was to dig into those mounds and explain in mathematical terms what was going on. His modest salary was paid by the U.S. government through the National Science Foundation.

Years later, his colleagues told me that my father was the first to realize how hemoglobin (the iron-containing protein in the red blood cells of vertebrates) carries oxygen to the lungs and releases it in bodily tissues where it is needed, and how this is facilitated and accelerated by the changing shape of the molecule. This process became known as "allostery"; because of Father's work, it can be used to explain a broad range of molecular activities. One possible application is to be able to predict how therapeutic compounds might interact with proteins in the body—in effect, to forecast drug-delivery pathways. To this day, scientists are doing experiments to test out this possibility. Some said that Father's work deserved a Nobel Prize. But, if such a thought crossed his mind, he never mentioned it.

My father was neither the first nor alone in his pursuit. As early as 1904, Danish physiologist Christian Bohr had described how oxygen molecules can snap (somewhat like Velcro) onto the heme molecule in the lungs and then be carried through the body to be released where they are needed—for example, in a runner's legs. There, the behavior is reversed; the oxygen is swapped for carbon dioxide, which is returned and discharged in the lungs. During this process the heme molecule actually twists itself into an S-curve, literally hooking itself around the oxygen or carbon dioxide molecules in order to transport them. But Bohr could not explain the details of this process.

Earlier still, in the 1870s, James Clerk Maxwell, founder of the Cavendish Laboratory at Cambridge University, had used mathematical equations to express linked relationships in the physical world. While Father's academic training was in biology, his familiarity with physics and growing interest in math helped him see new connections between these nineteenth-century mathematical concepts and the twentieth-century challenge of explaining how hemoglobin worked. In fact, one of his earliest scientific papers, published in 1937, had probed the relationship between hemoglobin's oxygen-binding affinity and electrical changes in the related hydrogen ions.

But his epiphany came in 1950, during the six months he spent in Japan. Brooding on this problem while on a visit to the Ryoanji Zen Garden in Kyoto he realized that hemoglobin's ability to bind oxygen was the result of its capacity to change shape. The following year, back at Harvard, he and David W. Allen, a graduate student, collaborated on a paper describing how oxygen binding at one site changed the overall shape of hemoglobin, much like the opening and closing of a fist, speeding the change. Furthermore, there were four sites on the hemoglobin molecule where binding could occur— and once oxygen had bound itself to one of those sites, the other three were more receptive to binding as well. What Father recognized, as he explained it later, was that the impact of oxygen binding to the first site increased the affinity of the other sites to also take on oxygen. It was, he said, like "putting your finger in a balloon—everything changes."

He condensed his insights into a scientific paper, a critical step in the world of science for an idea to achieve recognition among peers. But getting that paper published was difficult. Enrico di Cera, a professor of biochemistry and biophysics at Washington University in St. Louis who became friends with my father in the 1980s, recalls that one obstacle was that "Jeffries was talking about conformational transitions, which [his scientific peers considered] was totally nuts!" Ultimately the paper did get published in the *Journal of Polymer Science*, which unfortunately was little read by biologists and biochemists. Moreover, many who did read it were alienated by the dense mathematical language my father used to express his ideas. But, said di Cera, "Those who waded through the math were rewarded by the first theoretical statement of 'allostery.'"

Today allostery is used as a tool to help understand how enzymes turn sugar into energy, how hormones or drugs enter cells, and how the normal functions of proteins can lead to disease when regulatory controls go awry. The 1951 article is a classic, says Guido Guidotti, a professor of biochemistry at Harvard University, "because it provided the first clues to how molecules respond to their environment by changing shape, and therefore how they function."

During his twenty-five years in Rome, Father was not only in contact with hemoglobin specialists, but he also began to renew relationships with scientists he had known in the past. By 1963 he was engaged in a plan proposed by Nobelist John Kendrew (soon to become "Sir John") to create what, in 1967, became the European Molecular Biology Organization. Known as EMBO, the organization's purpose was to help build what was then a tiny field of research into the giant it is today by bringing together researchers from across the continent. Father became the organization's first Secretary General, a member of its governing Council and a member of almost every committee established by the Council.

More importantly, he reestablished a connection with the biologist Jacques Monod, a member of the Institut Pasteur in Paris, whom he had known when he was at the embassy a decade earlier. Monod already had surged to prominence when he and another French researcher, Francois Jacob, did much to explain how genes

regulate cell metabolism by directing the biosynthesis of enzymes—
work that won them the Nobel Prize in Physiology or Medicine in
1965. Now, Monod and the young researcher Jean-Pierre Changeux
were in the process of formulating a theory to explain changes in the
binding affinity of an enzyme. Their finding became known as the
"two-state model," because it postulated that an enzyme molecule,
which is a form of protein, was always in either a "tense" or a
"relaxed" state. In the tense state, also known as a "binding" state, the
enzyme could grab onto another molecule—in the case of hemoglobin that would be oxygen or carbon dioxide—and carry it to where
it was needed. In the relaxed state, the enzyme molecule would have
straightened itself out to release its cargo. Monod and Changeux
thought their model might have broad applications.

But, as Robert W. Noble recalled it, theirs was far from a finished
product. Noble received his doctorate in biophysics at the Massachusetts Institute of Technology in 1964 and in the autumn of that
year began working as a "postdoc" research fellow at Regina Elena,
just as my father was beginning his collaboration with Monod and
Changeux. "They had a wonderful idea," Noble remembered, but
were not able to express it well for others. "They could draw pictures
and explain verbally that it ought to work this way," he said. "But
they didn't know how to write it down."

And this is where Father's role became vital. Indeed, it was
almost as if this day was predestined to arrive in his lifetime. As others have since noted, Institut Pasteur and Regina Elena represented
two quite different scientific cultures. Coming from his own perspective, Father recognized, as his collaborators apparently did not,
that what they were seeing reflected fundamental laws of physics,
namely the laws of thermodynamics, and that these observations
could be described mathematically.

"With Jeffries' calculations you could write out the equation,"
Noble said. And with an equation in hand, other researchers
were now able to postulate outcomes that could be tested in the

laboratory and then either explained or discarded on the basis of solid numbers.

Yes, blood and particularly hemoglobin were a lifelong passion for him. Brunori, his colleague in Rome, remembers him once referring to this macromolecule as "a beautiful woman" who is always "fascinating and ever so attractive." But in the end, the cold, hard, immutable laws of physics prevailed.

In May 1965, barely a year after Father began collaborating with Monod and Changeux, their research was published in the *Journal of Molecular Biology* under the title "On the Nature of Allosteric Transitions: A Plausible Model." The paper runs for thirty printed pages and is virtually unfathomable to anyone without solid grounding in mathematics. My father was listed as the second author, and the so-called MWC paper has become a standby in the field. Allosteric theory not only can be used to describe interactions with proteins, but it connects other factors, including such environmental ones as acidity or temperature, to changes that are observed in the laboratory.

Almost a half-century after its publication the model expressed in this paper remains the subject of intense study and experimentation. I have been told that it is one of the most frequently cited research publications in the history of biochemistry and molecular biology. A copy that I saw in the Science Library at the Massachusetts Institute of Technology is well thumbed and soiled from repeated reading—surely a testament to its importance. The equations Father wrote are, as Bob Noble put it, "a foundation tool" for the study of molecular biology. Before, researchers could only record their observations and wonder. Thanks to my father, Noble said, the MWC paper "allows you to make measurements about the binding of drugs to receptors, and then to interpret the results quantitatively"—a necessity for research to move forward.

In May 2005, Brunori and a few others organized a symposium in Rome to celebrate the fortieth anniversary of the MWC paper's publication. The day-long meeting was held in the Accademia Nazionale dei Lincei near Trastevere on the right bank of the Tiber River. The Lincei, housed in a huge yellow building with double staircases and a garden of palm trees, is Italy's premier organization of scientists, similar to the National Academy of Sciences in the United States, the Académie Française in France and Britain's independent science academy known simply as the Royal Society. Father was a member of the Lincei while he was in Rome and had a room there in which to work when he became too frail to cross town to the Regina Elena. There were nineteen invited participants from six countries, including Israel and Switzerland. The nine speakers included Changeux, still with the Institut Pasteur, and di Cera from St. Louis.

The symposium's title was "Allosteric Proteins: 40 Years with Monod-Wyman-Changeux." The sponsoring committee, including Brunori and Changeux, noted in the introduction to their program that the MWC paper quickly became "one of the most exciting and cited publications" in the history of biochemistry and molecular biology. Moreover, they wrote, the paper's importance was now far broader than ever expected. "For many years the allosteric theory was applied, by-and-large, to hemoglobin and a handful of enzymes. But more recently it was demonstrated to account for the behaviour of many other proteins, sometimes very complex, such as receptors, chaperonins and multiprotein complexes. Allostery has become an acquired concept which is extensively covered in all Biochemistry textbooks."

The meeting's stated purpose was to discuss both the validity and limits of the allosteric theory when applied to complex proteins and to assess where future research might lead. Presentations began with a discussion, led by Changeux, of "The MWC model in retrospect; from regulatory enzymes to receptor channels." They ended with dissertations on "Intra-protein electronic transfer," by Israel Pecht from the Weizmann Institute in Rehovot, and "Allosteric states in multi-protein complexes," by physicist Thomas Duke of England's Cavendish Laboratory. Almost all of it was incomprehensible to me, but my impression was that, while this work has not yet produced a cure for cancer, the theory is quite alive and scientists are still testing its limits. Changeux, for one, has come to believe that the MWC model of protein interactions can be applied also to understanding the behavior of neurons in the brain.

⋯

My father's work did not end with the publication of the MWC treatise. Another notable paper, though less noticed, was published in 1967 in the *Journal of the American Chemical Society*. In it he presented a detailed discussion of the equations involved and used the term "allosteric binding potential," advancing toward the concept that the allosteric properties seen in hemoglobin could also be found in other enzymes and proteins. And, in the ensuing years, Father continued to devise mathematical models for other cooperative proteins, often working with his friend Stanley J. Gill, a biochemistry professor at the University of Colorado in Boulder. Over the course of eleven years they wrote a textbook titled *Binding and Linkage: Functional Chemistry of Biological Macromolecules*. Three hundred and thirty pages long and full of graphs and formulas, it was published in 1990, when my father was eighty-nine years old. Gill, who was exactly my own age, died the following year at sixty-two. Almost two decades later this book is still in print and is still regarded as a cornerstone of modern biophysical chemistry. It is widely used in graduate courses, and, as an aside, I will add that it still produces modest royalties every year.

Father's work did not go unrecognized. Among the honors accorded him were nominations to the prestigious National

Academy of Sciences, America's top science organization, and the American Academy of Arts and Sciences, as well as his membership in Italy's Lincei. Paying tribute to him eight years after his death, the National Academy commissioned publication of a biographical memoir, written by di Cera along with Robert A. Alberty, emeritus professor of chemistry at the Massachusetts Institute of Technology. The fact that he was nominated to those academies was noteworthy, they wrote. "But the important thing," they added, "was that he was sought out by biochemists around the world for advice and collaboration."

Thick with details about Father's many-layered life, their fourteen-page memoir delivers some of its highest praise for some of his earliest work, particularly the paper he wrote in 1951 with Allen—the first time that he applied his knowledge of physics and the unchangeable laws of thermodynamics to a biological question. Tucked away in a relatively obscure scientific journal and little read by those who should have read it, that paper constituted *de facto* the discovery of allostery long before Monod and Jacob formulated their concepts at the Institut Pasteur. "Even today," di Cera and Alberty wrote, "very few biophysicists and biochemists are fully aware of the contribution that this seminal work had in the development of allosteric theory."

Recalling that Father once had remarked (to di Cera) that one should "never yield to temptation, unless it persists," they declared: "Thermodynamics was his lifelong temptation, and Wyman's monumental contribution was to bring the rigor of thermodynamics to biochemistry."

Chapter 18

Haute Borne

The first time I saw Haute Borne was in August 1980. Father and Olga had been there off and on for just over eight years. My brother Jeff had made a Christmas visit in 1975, during an eighteen-month period when he was working in Holland, but I had been tied up elsewhere. Now I was driving down from Paris, a distance of about 100 kilometers, with my Boston cousin Diana Stainow.

As Di and I traveled, the country opened into farmland with increasingly small villages nestled among copses of gnarled oaks. We left the highway for Chéroy and Saint-Valérien and the road narrowed. The last stretch, heading toward the market town of Pont-sur-Yonne, was no more than a lane twisting through vast whaleback hills, planted with wheat and sunflowers. Here and there piles of turnips waited by the road to be lugged off to market. And in the distance, against the trees, we could see an occasional church spire.

The name, *La Haute Borne*, means "the high boundary marker." We stumbled on the marker itself and turned right on an even smaller road. Around a blind corner was a green wooden fence marking the old farm. Father opened the big gates that enclosed the yard. Di and I had arrived in time for lunch, served, as always in those days, at a primitive round table under a plum tree outside the long low house.

It was Olga's younger sister, Marina, who had found the place through a Russian friend who had a cottage nearby. Until his death she had shared its ownership with her cousin, Pierre Romanoff. Originally, I suppose, a French farmer had owned the surrounding fields. Now those belonged to a Polish family named Rado, and the vast fields, which M. Rado mowed in a cloud of dust, were part of the surrounding landscape. Several times a week the Rados' daughter, Lilie, would come by with milk and cream from their farm and do odd jobs around the house. From time to time, Simeon, an old Cossack, whose horse had been shot from under him during the Russian Revolution, would bicycle over from Saint-Valérien with his dog, Violette, in the basket, to mow the lawn and help clip the hawthorne hedge.

At the time Diana and I made our visit, Olga, Marina and Father would have been the only residents, unless Olga's granddaughter, Marie, was there for riding lessons during the school holidays. But the place often was full of guests—Russian friends from Paris, scientists from Italy, England or America and, as now, occasional relatives from Boston. At the age of seventy-nine my father had taken to spending the three summer months at Haute Borne, often returning at Christmas and New Year's as well.

Father was anxious to show us the "improvements" he and Olga had made to Marina's establishment. The house with its row of open glass doors and white shutters sat behind a bank of lawn and flowers, and they were planting trees around the edge of the property to keep out the prevailing winds. A "grange" or barn included three bedrooms and a dismal bathroom. Di and I slept in the upstairs bedrooms, above a room full of preserves, drying fruit and piled deck chairs. Casement windows overlooked the fields and vegetable garden, and at night I would get out of the monster bed that Olga had found at some junk sale to watch big thunderstorms racing over the ripening wheat. The main building faced the lawn and distant fields at right angles to the grange. It consisted of the kitchen; the small parlor with its big fireplace, two sofa-beds and television set; and Marina's bedroom and bath. These led into the old two-story cow shed, which Father had converted into a second, grand parlor with another big fireplace and a steep staircase leading to a narrow balcony and the long loft. Up there, Father had turned the end room into a study. Olga had lined their slope-ceilinged bedroom and a guest alcove with printed cloth. The bathroom had a skylight and a tub so narrow that Olga wouldn't use it and Father had rigged a rope to pull himself out.

All in all, it was charming. And for the next two weeks my father was the perfect host, taking Di and me on daylong picnics to the surrounding villages with their manor houses, Romanesque churches, tiny shops and gardens. Once or twice we went to the big open market outside the cathedral in the nearby city of Sens. Other times we went to the riverside village of Pont-sur-Yonne, where Olga insisted on stopping for strong coffee in the little square and local shoppers crowded by us in search of fresh tomatoes, cheap suitcases and gauzy shirts.

By the end of that first visit I knew the countryside fairly well. That would stand me in good stead on future trips when I would be left to my own devices as my father got increasingly into his routine of writing in the morning, napping after lunch and walking in the late afternoon. From then on, I would visit Haute Borne each summer, often sharing the time with Dimitri and his family.

Meanwhile, Father was anything but inactive. He and Stan Gill were working on *Binding and Linkage*, which Father described then as "a little book." When the project began in 1979, Father was already

Olga's son Dimitri with his wife, Eliane, at Haute Borne, France, about 1980. (Author photo.)

suffering increasingly from Parkinson's and still had traces of the dizziness caused by Meniere's disease. But he was still clambering around the hills outside Rome with Alfredo Colosimo. Three years earlier, he and others, including Maurizio Brunori, had spent the summer researching fish hemoglobin with an expedition on the Amazon organized by his former Harvard tutee, Austen Riggs, now a University of Texas neurobiologist. During one of his yearly visits to Colorado to collaborate with Gill they walked together down the steep Bright Angel Trail into the Grand Canyon.

He continued, too, to dash from Rome to Paris or to Boston, and from there back to Switzerland or Haute Borne, largely on business. In May of 1980 he spent a weekend on the island of Elba; in July that year he went with Olga to a scientific meeting in Romania, where he was treated as an elder statesman. A year later Father attended an International Biophysical Congress in Mexico where a special symposium was held to honor his eightieth birthday, and in September 1981 he took Olga on a ten-day visit to Moscow and Tblisi for more scientific meetings. In May of the following year he was in Boston for my brother's wedding, at age fifty, to Margaret Grealey. She was the second oldest in an Irish farm family of twelve children, and Father wrote, "I sometimes wonder what Grandpa Wyman would think of Jeff marrying an Irish Roman Catholic—better not to think."

His interest in art also was as keen as ever. In the fall of 1981, he went to a large exhibit of Turner watercolors in Paris. "They were extraordinarily beautiful, with all the lace-like detail and his piercing blues and reds," he wrote. "In a way he makes me think of Cezanne. For me they are the greatest figures in the world of visual arts since 1800. Each is pressing steadily towards a goal, always you feel unachieved but recognizable. That is something lacking in Picasso, that chameleon-like painter for whom things were too easy."

As he moved into his eighties, though, my father was beginning to feel old. "When one gets to my age," he wrote on March 22, 1980, "everything seems to take ten times as long as it used to, even dressing or eating, to say nothing of writing and trying to solve some problems. Old Simeon at Haute Borne is two or three years older than I and even slower. He complains of not being able to fasten his smaller buttons and he can no longer mow the lawn, though he still looks after the house."

Nevertheless, Father's research grant from the National Science Foundation was renewed for two more years. "I shall be about eighty-two when it comes to an end," he noted. Two years before that he had written, "Sometimes I feel I should not be too sorry if it were not renewed and I were to start taking things more quietly." Yet with the NSF contract now signed he would be returning to Rome in the fall. "I am getting to the age where I rather resent these constant moves and uprootings but in the end I find they are always good for me and give me a fresh point of view," he wrote. A year later, in October 1981, he looked back on his summer's travels as "a shaking up which did me a lot of good and has helped me to see things I have been working on in a larger way."

But things were slowing down whether Father liked it or not. In a letter written on Thanksgiving Day in 1981, he reported that "I have changed my life style quite drastically since we got back to Rome about three weeks ago. I used to go up to the university every morning with Cora [his secretary] and come back for lunch, either with her or by bus. Now I have arranged for the use of a very large room just across the river from my apartment in the building belonging to Accademia Lincei, of which I am a member. So I spend most of my mornings and sometimes afternoons there instead of making the tiresome trip through Roman traffic to the other side of the city. I do still go to the lab once or twice a week but no more. My room is a large one with a huge long table and walls lined with books from the library of Levi-Civita, one of the great Italian mathematicians of the last century. It is a splendid place to write and think, surrounded by those books, flooded by sunshine and quiet as the grave." That December he wrote that he had no car in Rome. "I don't like driving anymore, in fact I no longer have a driving license."

That year I left my job as editor of the *Globe*'s editorial page, which I had held for five years, and began writing monthly articles on ideas, some of which were rather daunting. Perhaps urged by Olga to be more responsive and perhaps because he was in a reflective mood, Father took an active interest in this. He asked about an article I had written on postmodern architecture that involved his old friend Philip Johnson. He also wanted to know about a piece I did on computers and artificial intelligence: "Brains are certainly computers, though perhaps not very fast or good ones, but are computers brains?" He wondered, as did Marvin Minsky of M.I.T. when I once interviewed him, whether computers would ever be able to make jokes.

His letters now were full of advice and commentary. Writing from Haute Borne on July 27, 1981, he answered my writer's dilemma. "I know what you mean about trying to go too deep. I have somewhat the same trouble in writing scientific things. I want to make them too precise and too general at the cost of great effort and delay. It is an admirable fault but one should remember that if one tries too hard to be precise (like the lawyers) it may be unintelligible. It is better to err on the side of simplicity and be more relaxed."

He commiserated with me on being in the dumps. "I too have moods of doubt and confusion when it seems that all I have done is either obvious and banal or else unsound. Then in the small hours of the morning, when it is still pitch black, comes my demon who takes advantage of my half-wakefulness to pose the most tormenting questions. But afterwards, when the sun is up and the morning dew is sparkling, I sit on the bench in the garden and everything changes."

He was interested too in world affairs. He deplored President Jimmy Carter's indecisive "Sunday school approach" to foreign policy and referred to him as "poor Carter." He thought Israel was causing trouble in the Middle East and would lose support if it continued to "flout international opinion." British Prime Minister Margaret Thatcher's economic policy, he wrote, "is based on a quite appealing monetarist philosophy but seems to be failing. So are all the other policies based on reason. I suppose it is because people do not act rationally so it is not to be expected that any rational plan will work." He was reading Dostoyevsky's *The Possessed* and found it "very relevant to our times." He was shocked that "books cost fifteen to sixteen dollars" and a meal in Paris ran to "about thirty dollars." By November 1982, however, the French franc had fallen from less than 4 to the dollar to 7.35, a source of political trouble in France but an advantage to him since he lived on his American money.

But bad news was coming from Rome. He had heard that the Patrizzi family, who owned the flat at 51 Piazza Farnese, might want the apartment back. Worse still was word that Eraldo Antonini, who had drawn Father to Rome and kept him there, had been diagnosed with lung cancer at the age of fifty-three. He died in the spring of 1983. Father and Olga moved permanently to Paris three years later in 1986. And while they continued returning to Haute Borne, Father was no longer able to dig and plant in the garden or scythe the edges of the lawn. His war with the moles, which he treated with "rat-bane" and fierce jabs with a pitchfork into their holes, was over. Now eighty-three, he walked with a stoop and carried a tall stick.

In Paris they moved into an old flat, owned by Olga's family, that was within sight of the Champ de Mars and the Eiffel Tower. Shortly after their arrival Olga advertised in *Le Figaro* for a helper and found Rukmal Wijesuria, a twenty-five-year-old man from Sri Lanka. Soon there was a collection of helpers—Augusto Domaresque, Iko, Hebert and Nilton, all from Brazil—who lived in the flat and took care of everyone. I remember Augusto especially for his love of cooking, flower arranging and jazz. "The boys" took turns buying groceries, cooking meals, going to the bank and cleaning the house. They slept in the flat, ate with the family, kept peace between Marina and Olga, made Father laugh and knew the whole circle of visitors who floated in and out of the household like a Russian circus.

Among my favorite visitors were Olga's brother Alexei and his dazzling, funny wife Marishka; tall, excitable Bernard Fonlladosa, who took us all on excursions and argued religion with Father; and Xenia Ouvaroff, the descendant of a general in the Battle of Borodino, who loved food, drink and gossip. The house was awhirl with White Russians: Natasha Kolsakoff, who guarded Marina; Lydie and Joseph, who were elegant even at Haute Borne; Tania and Aline, Polish twins who were always in trouble; the woman from upstairs who came to see Olga in patent-leather spike-heels with her toy poodle. Somehow they all seemed more excitable and exciting than Father's old friends from America.

⁘

One summer day in the late 1980s, my father took off for a walk through the big field in front of the house at Haute Borne. He fell on the uneven mud road and couldn't get up. Monsieur Rado, at work with his combine, found him and carried him home in his arms. Father had broken his hip. I flew from Boston and Olga took me to see him at the hospital in Sens. The sides of his bed were raised but Father had got over the rails the night before and fallen onto the floor. I think both Olga and I believed he would die. His eyes were closed and his face was the color of egg whites. I remember I couldn't stand it and rushed into town and bought a box of fancy dark chocolates. Father, who loved fudge, came to in a flash and was

Augusto pushing Father uphill at Haute Borne before his afternoon nap. (Author photo.)

soon back at home, though it turned out he had broken the other hip too.

After that he was stuck in a wheelchair. But the boys took him into the garden every day. Rukmal would push him gently up the slope to his long chair under the plum tree. Or Augusto would tip the chair up on its back wheels and hurtle my father, laughing delightedly, to his afternoon perch among the bees and the vines.

In the evening we would all sit out of the wind, near the grange, and sip gin and tonics, of which Olga disapproved. One night we were there when a huge bird flew overhead, giving a scream. It was "Le Grand Duc," an owl that thumps around by day in attics and lofts. His terrible cry was designed to scare the mice into running out through the cut wheat.

That night and every night at Haute Borne, Marina insisted on a ceremonial locking up. The big gate was barred and the white shutters were secured from inside. Alone upstairs in the grange, I would lean out the casement window and watch for dawn.

Chapter 19

Twilight

The Paris flat, when Father and Olga moved there in 1986, was just as it had been since Olga's parents had bought it in 1945. Just as it had been when Father first described it in a letter to me dated December 30, 1962. Just as it was when I had donated $500 to have the big parlor repainted in 1966. Olga's mother had died in 1959 and I never saw her. But her father was still alive when I visited 29 Avenue la Motte Piquet in 1971. Now he too was gone, along with Pierre Romanoff, a retired test pilot and cousin, who had lived with the family for many years and whom Marina had finally married as he lay dying of leukemia in 1969.

Until Father and Olga arrived from Rome, Marina had been living alone in the flat with only her dog, Mir, for companionship. It had seemed almost a good deed for them to join her. Aside from his Parkinson's, which was an increasing liability, Father was well at the time. And, although they fought, Olga and Marina had successfully shared the place at Haute Borne for the past sixteen summers. Now Marina was getting increasingly deaf, Olga had stomach problems and a bad heart, and at eighty-five Father was already frail. I had seldom visited Rome but now I made almost yearly trips to Paris.

An early visit in 1990 was typical. The night plane from Boston would arrive at Roissy at dawn and I would get to Avenue la Motte Piquet by nine in the morning, crossing the Alexander III bridge to Les Invalides, then driving up the old wide street to the circle at École Militaire. If I had the code for the door, which frequently changed, I would punch it in and someone would come onto the interphone and let me through the pair of heavy glass doors into the tiled lobby with stairs spiraling out of sight. Waiting by the small wheezy elevator on the fifth floor, Rukmal would kiss both my cheeks, like a French cousin, and lead me down the cluttered hall, past the double drawing room with its view of the top of the Eiffel Tower, and around the corner past the dark little kitchen to the single room where Father waited.

Olga, who stayed up late reading, was still asleep in her parents' old room in the back part of the flat. But Marina swished along in her slippers and dressing gown, gray hair astray, to greet me. Father was sitting with a breakfast tray on his lap—often smoked salmon and cheese on fresh bread. The boys had rigged a board across the tub in Father's adjoining bathroom where he could sit while he was being washed and shaved. Now dressed, he wore a bib over his old sweater and the baggy sweatpants that were all he could comfortably wear. A small segment of rubber tubing served as a kind of home-made straw to suck up his morning tea and, interchangeably, his wine at dinner.

"Well, there you are," he would say. "How was the trip?" Rukmal had brought me a cup of chicory coffee, then left. And Father asked about the matter of a family trustee, something that had been on his mind for more than a year. "Aunt Susan thinks it's unwise to pick one of your cousins in case the trustee-cousin doesn't work out."

I looked around at the familiar room with the wild wallpaper that Father had chosen himself, the cream and white table stacked with his papers, and Olga's big armchair by the casement window. The window was open now to a light breeze and a watery sun. Olga would close it when she came in.

And here's how the day went: About eleven Rukmal arrived to take Father for his morning "walk." Bundled into a shapeless overcoat, an old tweed hat on his head, Father was hoisted out of his deep chair and shifted to the two aluminum elbow canes he was still able to use. Then, with Rukmal at his side, he would totter toward the elevator and out onto the street.

The old neighborhood had become prosperous, I thought, as I looked into a shop selling riding boots and hats and another selling paintings and prints. One window was full of old medals and military decorations. I had seen such displays on other visits to Paris and wondered again about the veterans who had been forced to sell these trophies of their past, men like Olga's father, perhaps. Once a member of the Tsar's inner circle, old Mr. Lodigensky had driven a taxi and rolled his own cigarettes to get by in wartime Paris.

Ahead of me, Father progressed slowly along the sidewalk on his canes. Rukmal stayed near but tactfully did not help until we came to one of the green benches on the broad sidewalk between the big street and the row of parked cars. Rukmal and I talked about such things as how to get to the bank, what he and Augusto did on their time off, events in the news. Father saved his breath until we reached the tiny park around the corner from Les Invalides. Once settled near the laurels, he happily reminisced about the prewar days when he taught at Harvard and my mother had been alive, about the huge Thanksgiving parties at Grandma Cabot's, about the sailing picnics in Maine, about the afternoon horseback rides on Naushon.

And through it all there had been expeditions on foot, a long trip to Norway with Mother, shorter outings with Jeffy and me. I thought of how fast Father had walked in his heyday, had an image of trailing him up a mountainside near their chalet in Switzerland, remembered the family story of the Scottish gillie who saw him start off at his breakneck pace and said, "He'll no last the day." Pretty soon the canes wouldn't be enough; Olga was already talking about a wheelchair. Soon they would build an addition to the back of the house in Haute Borne so Father and one of the boys could sleep on the ground floor.

No one was in the flat when we got back. The noon sun poured into Father's room, casting shadows across his watercolor paintings, one of mountains and a palm tree above Lake Como and another of a field in France with pink grasses leading away to a forest like the one at Haute Borne. A small oil of the Tsar and another of a wooded path in the Crimea, both done by Mr. Lodigensky, hung on the other walls. Over the table-desk hung a painting by Jeffy of a sailboat rounding a stormy headland and my little watercolor of the Pulpit Rock at North Haven, both recent tributes to Father's far greater skill. Rukmal went to the kitchen to make lunch. I sat on the end of Father's austere single bed.

"What do you think we should do about this apartment?" he asked unexpectedly.

I drew back. He was asking me, and he really wanted my advice. I was deeply pleased but knew I must be careful. He didn't have much choice; the sisters might listen to him but they would really decide themselves. He was at their mercy now.

"If I were you," I said, "I'd try to stay here. You have this nice room where you're out of the way, where you can work if you want to. Your friends can come to visit you here. And you have the boys to take care of you. Besides, if you and Olga moved out, Marina would be alone again. Because Rukmal and Augusto would go too, wouldn't they?"

"Oh yes," he said. "They would go if we go." I thought he sounded sad and tired.

"Do you think you could manage in the smaller room?" I asked. "Is there a way you could switch around within this flat?"

In fact I didn't see how it could be done. The back rooms were down a small flight of steps; the hall was taken up now with built-in cupboards. Father needed the bathroom that Olga had carved out of his bedroom. He needed a place where his scientist friends could come and call on him, where Jeffy and I and other connections from his American past could get away from the hubbub of visiting Russians and the constant battles between the two sisters, usually over nothing important.

As if he could read my mind, Father said, "Marina is very jealous of the people who come here to see me. I am afraid she feels left out, though Olga and I always urge our friends to go in and talk to her."

I was shocked to hear my father talking of jealousy. That was the kind of personal emotion he never discussed. Emotions were something, maybe like pain, that didn't count in his order of things. Perhaps *jealous* wasn't the right word. This had been Marina's home until Father and Olga chose to move in with her. Now they each had a room of their own, while Marina slept on a couch off the parlor. Although a notorious tightwad, Father was paying most of the rent and repairs, both at Haute Borne and in Paris. But I wondered, angrily, if that was enough.

We heard voices in the hall. Olga came into the room and we kissed. "You had a good trip? And you had a nice walk together, Jeffiki?" Over the years Olga had become blowsy. Still she managed to look like a tragedy queen as she sat in the big chair by the window, her Slavic blue eyes flashing at Father as she talked. For thirty years she had played the role of Attendant Slave to the Great Scientist. Now she had pride of place as his nurse and protector.

I should be grateful, I thought. I couldn't do it myself. And with his time running out, I had to accept that my father and I would never paddle a double kayak together as we had once done for ten days in Finland. He would never again be able to cross the Atlantic for visits with me and Jeffy in Boston. We could still gossip about life and old times, but it was unlikely now that he would ever say the magic words that would tell me I had measured up to his goals. He was making his final escape and it made me feel lonely and sad.

While Father slept after lunch, I would go off to visit some museum he had selected for me. But, without him to keep me there, I seldom stayed for more than an hour. One afternoon when he had sent me across town to the Museum of African and Oceanic Art, I came back and described a wooden head that was almost choked with bronze coils around the neck, the face serene and remote above the stifling necklace.

"Oh yes, I remember her," Father said. Then he asked about other objects in parts of the museum that I had missed. "Too bad," he said. "Those things are among the finest they have." In spite of myself, I felt my mission had failed.

+++

Because of the shortage of space at the flat, I was staying at a small hotel around the corner. I would go back there to have a bath and read before returning to Father for dinner. By then, Augusto or one of the other boys would have replaced Rukmal for the next twenty-four-hour shift. The house smelled of frying onions, another meal of curried chicken or veal stew. Someone had found half a bottle of gin in the icebox; I had bought tonic across the street. Father had often told me in Boston that I drank too much but, during my visit, he joined me in a ceremonial cocktail. Mixing his gin and tonic, I tried not to make it too strong. Olga, who never drank even wine because of her heart or her ulcers, believed alcohol gave Father nightmares.

I would bring a tray into the big cluttered parlor. Marina would be in her corner armchair, with her dog by her side and, upon the low round table at her feet, a waxed tablet for people to write to her when she could not hear their shouted comments.

Often the sisters' brother Alexei would join us for drinks with his wife. Alexei had worked in America and Marishka presently worked for the Bishop of the American Episcopal Church in Paris, so both spoke fluent English. Marishka had terrible arthritis in her hands and a way of gasping as she talked, as if what she was saying were too exciting or too funny.

As I listened, I thought of something Father had written to me in 1959, when he and Olga were wandering in Europe. "What extraordinary people they all are, these Russians! Some streak runs through them all—from Khrushchev to the old aristocracy—much genius, great warmth, much indigence and untidiness but still power of organization, enormous patriotism and esprit de corps, moods and passions, frankness and kindliness which does not exclude cunning and intrigue, unbounded hospitality and profligality, tremendous capacity for love, devotion and hate. They are just like the people in the novels, which don't exaggerate by one letter."

In that hour or so before supper, there were always visitors. Claude and Armel Debru, who lived with their three young children near Les Invalides, were among the most frequent. Claude was writing a history of science that dealt at length with Father's work. Armel, dark and intense as a sparrow, had been born in Romania and cooed over Father even more than Olga. A particular favorite was Bernard Fonlladosa, the father of four adult sons, who knew every twist and turn of the household at La Motte Piquet. Though he understood English, Bernard spoke only French. He was full of jokes and advice on every subject, defended an arcane view of Catholicism, and was the only person, other than Olga and Rukmal, allowed to drive Father in Paris. It was typical that, when he took us

169

to the Guimet Museum of Asian Art behind the Trocadero, Bernard was able to park and get Father in by the back door.

Bernard or one of the other visitors usually stayed on for supper. The oval table between the two drawing rooms was set with cloth napkins in pouches embroidered by Dimitri's wife, Eliane, with the names of household members and the most frequent guests. Augusto and Rukmal had these napkin holders but I never did. Olga and I would help bring in the meal. Augusto assisted Father to his seat at the far end of the table. Behind him, on a mantelpiece with a large gold-framed mirror over it, stood a bowl of silk flowers in a glass jar, half-filled with water to make them seem real. Over a side table was another, more formal portrait of Tsar Nicholas.

After a brief flutter of polite conversation, the talk turned to earlier discussions of domestic details. Seated next to me, Marina spoke in her deaf-person's high metallic voice, while her hearing aid wheezed in her bosom and the television rattled on, unattended, behind my chair. I found it hard to understand her, although she spoke English as well as French and Russian, and my responses to

Dimitri discussing family matters with Bernard Fonlladosa (in white) in Father's Paris flat. (Photographer unknown; collection of the author.)

her questions had to be transmitted by one of the boys. My father's frail voice did not penetrate at all and he had given up even trying to talk to his sister-in-law.

Olga scarcely touched her food and got up during every meal to fetch something, take plates away, or answer the hall telephone, whose ring would trigger a flashing light to alert Marina if she were alone in the house. Marina was deaf but not blind, and Olga took pleasure in telling me that her sister had recently spotted the husband of a friend of mine in the bar next door with another woman. Mean of Olga to pass it on, I thought. It must have been she who told Father that Marina had had a romance with a German officer during the war; the officer of course was married and returned to Germany, presumably to the relief of the Lodigenskys.

Sometimes, when Father was asleep or busy, Marina and I would watch tennis or equestrian events on the TV. And sometimes we were able to converse. Once, she told me, she had become suspicious of a Russian who had applied for an American visa through the refugee bureau at the French Foreign Office where she still worked. And, lo and behold, he turned out to be a known spy. Another time, during the war, Marina heard that the part of Paris where her parents lived had been bombed. She rushed from her office, stole an unlocked bicycle and pedaled across the city to find that all was well. But when she returned, she discovered that the bike belonged to a Nazi colonel. Luckily the bike had not been missed.

I admired Marina and hated to think of her being squashed by Father and Olga. She never said so, but I thought Marina felt left out by Olga's obsession with my father. He was distant, an intrusive presence, but Marina wanted to protect him too. On the other hand, I think they brought a new liveliness into her life. I remember Claude Debru telling me that his own life was "changed entirely by meeting Jeffries and Olga. It became more difficult but more interesting," he said, describing himself and Armel as "part of the Court." He added, "They had a big impact on people, each inspiring in their own way."

From the parlor, we could hear Augusto and Olga talking and laughing as they prepared my father for bed. I would go in and kiss him goodnight. Then Marina would walk me back to my hotel, guided by her dog, Mir, from curb to lamppost as we passed the restaurant on the corner where a waiter shucked oysters taken from bushels of ice. In my little hotel room I would reflect that, if you could bore a hole through the buildings, Father's bedroom was roughly 100 yards away.

My visits to Paris usually lasted about a week. Unlike Dimitri and Eliane, I was not expected to kiss the family icon before embarking on my possibly dangerous journey but, each time as I left, Olga would try to press on me some small memento. Once, moved to a similar gesture, Father asked if I would like a small figurine he had bought in Morocco. But, in the end, he decided he should keep it himself. It belonged with two other figures, he said, and it would be a shame to break up the set.

The Tsar presided from his canvas over our farewell dinner and Father sucked up an extra glass of wine through the green rubber tube. Marina invited me to visit them in the country and Olga reminded me to call Stan Gill in Boulder and "tell him your father is waiting to see him." Then Rukmal would take me and my bags to the taxi stand and I would be off.

Two weeks later I called Paris and asked Father how things were going. "We had a nice visit from Bernard. And your friend, Alice Furlaud, is coming tonight," he said.

"What about the flat?" I asked.

"What? Oh, nothing. It hasn't come up," he said.

Good, I thought. He has decided to wait it out. And he'll probably get his way, just as he's always done.

But I recalled Father's quavery voice and felt that now he, too, was vulnerable. Soon Rukmal or Augusto would be closing the curtains and windows and putting my father to bed.

Chapter 20

Sudden Loss

The telephone call from Paris came at four-thirty on the morning of Monday, January 9, 1990. Olga had been found on the bath-room floor, dead of a heart attack at the age of seventy-seven.

I was dumbfounded. Olga had talked endlessly about her health, refused to eat butter and cheese because of heartburn, never touched wine. But I'd always thought it was a bid for attention. It was my father, a dozen years older and crippled by Parkinson's, who should have died.

I caught a plane that night, checked into the little hotel nearby and got to the flat on Avenue La Motte Piquet at nine-fifteen. Dimitri and Eliane were already there, having driven all day across France from their home in Switzerland. Marina, herself seventy-five and completely deaf, was still asleep in the tiny room off the parlor. Lece, one of the three Brazilians who took care of my father by turns, was at work in the kitchen.

Dimitri gave me the familial triple kiss on the cheeks. "They are all right," he said.

I had a thousand questions. Would the household be able to manage without Olga? Should my father remain in the flat where the two sisters had comforted, entertained and fought each other over the years since World War II? I dreaded the thought of taking him back to Boston. How would I get him there and care for him if I did? My life and my job would be sidelined forever.

"Things can continue as they are," Dimitri reassured me. "The fewer changes now, the better. We can see again at Easter. For now they can manage. And I am only a few hours away in Fribourg."

He took me down the black-and-white tiled hall, past the kitchen and my father's room, past the bathroom where Olga had been found on the floor, past the door to the small room where Eliane was asleep, to the steps leading down to Olga's room at the back of the flat.

My stepmother was laid out on the bed, a fur rug over her body, her face white and peaceful. Her false teeth had been taken out and a

Olga and her granddaughter, Marie, having lunch in the garden at Haute Borne with Father in 1975. (Author photo.)

bandanna tied under her chin to keep the jaw from dropping. A small Russian icon was propped in her hands. A tall lamp shone on the old bureau to her left and another was lit on the wooden sideboard at the foot of the bed. The room was full of flowers and her necklaces hung like garlands over some small family pictures by the door. She would stay there until the funeral on Friday.

Much, much more shocking than the corpse was my father, hunched in a side chair by the drawn curtains. His face was puffy from medicine and his eyes, as he looked up to greet me, seemed red and tearful.

"It was so sudden," he said. "I keep thinking of things I want to tell her." I sat beside him in silence, full of pity but wondering where he would go from here.

It was a blustery day but Father wanted to go outdoors. The young Brazilian woman dressed him. She reminded me of Olga, making him wear a warm hat and tying a wool scarf around his neck. Claude Debru was waiting and the three of us crowded into the tiny elevator and descended from the fifth floor to the tiled vestibule where Father got into his wheelchair.

Olga had been dead only one day but the conversation turned to everyday matters. We stopped and looked at the little park-garden at the bottom of the street but didn't go in. Back, bumpety-bump over the curbs. Pushing the chair was not as easy as it looked. If you didn't back the chair down the curb or tip the front wheels up on the other side, Father could be thrown forward onto the pavement.

"You have to go at it straight on," Father said, unafraid.

After lunch Father napped as usual. Marina was reading or sleeping in her room off the green parlor. Dimitri took me to the little room, where we sat on the bed and talked. He was prepared to take charge of the family. Rukmal had returned to Sri Lanka, but one of the Brazilian boys would be the local major domo. "Augusto is very responsible, more capable than the others. He can do the shopping, everything." I was only half reassured. We discussed the fact that Father and Marina did not communicate. It was partly their mutual deafness, partly because Father never tried.

"It is too bad Jeffries didn't make more effort when he and my mother were first married," said Dimitri. "But it is too late to change that now." Perhaps they would get along better without Olga there to irritate Marina by fussing over Father all the time, I suggested. "Could be," said Dimitri.

When Father woke up he wanted to visit Olga. I went with him. In the darkened room someone had opened the windows against a nonexistent smell. Father was overcome with shaking tears. I held his hand and he held back—very tight and strong. Olga's parents had slept in this room but now it was quintessentially hers. The walls were hung with watercolors Father had painted at the country place where he had courted Olga forty years earlier. She had claimed the photo-montage of Father as a boy that I had made for them. Every surface was cluttered with small trinkets brought back from their life together in Egypt and Italy.

Beside me, Father suddenly recited from Tennyson's poem, "Break, Break, Break":

> O, well for the fisherman's boy,
> That he shouts with his sister at play!
> O, well for the sailor lad,
> That he sings in his boat on the bay!
>
> And the stately ships go on
> To their haven under the hill;
> But O for the touch of a vanish'd hand
> And the sound of a voice that is still! . . .

Then, his voice stronger, from Ecclesiastes:

> *Or ever the silver cord be loosed,*
> *Or the golden bowl broken,*
> *Or the pitcher be broken at the fountain,*
> *Or the wheel be broken at the cistern,*
> *And the dust return to the earth as it was,*
> *And the spirit return unto God who gave it.*

After a pause he said, "There's a feedback in grief, I suppose." I asked what he meant and he said, "Expressing grief makes you feel it more. I was brought up to believe that expressing feelings like grief was a sign of emotional weakness. Perhaps that's wrong." I told him I thought it was a mixture of wishing that grief would never end and fearing that catharsis would cut it short. "I remember your coming into my room to tell me that Mother had died, with tears pouring down your face. But I don't really remember much after that. I don't think we spent very much time grieving then. Maybe we should have."

"I left too soon," he said. "I think it hurt you and Jeffy."

I asked him whether he wanted to stay in Paris or come back to Boston. He answered, "Oh, stay, I think. When we came here, we thought we could all help each other. We knew one of us would die someday. None of us thought it would be Olga, of course. But Marina and I are dependent on each other now."

Augusto arrived at three. We were back in my father's room with its two armchairs on either side of the desk facing the door, the bureau and the single bed. The curtains by the high casement window billowed gently against the wild, jungly wallpaper my father loved. Father had once described Augusto, who was thin and blond, of Polish descent, as "the perfect Slav." As soon as he saw him, Father broke into tears, his mouth a terrible rectangle of mismatched teeth like a Japanese painting. Augusto walked right up to him, kissed him on both cheeks and put his forehead against my father's, holding the back of his head. Then the Brazilian crouched in front of him, holding my father's hands. I wished that I had been able to be so demonstrative.

Minutes later, we were out of the house again. Augusto took Father into the commercial garage next door to get air in the wheelchair's tires. They looked absurd coming out of the passage designed for trucks. Dimitri was with us and we crossed to the bank so that Father could sign a paper giving my stepbrother the right to cash checks on the two household accounts. He would give the cards to Augusto, who could draw up to $600 a week on each. Dimitri returned to the flat to meet the undertakers, who, he said, "would pack Olga's body in ice, inject it and so on."

Father, Augusto and I continued into the Champ de Mars, the big park that runs from the Eiffel Tower to the École Militaire. Father got out of the wheelchair and walked a short way on his canes. We sat on a bench. An old woman passed, scattering crumbs for the birds, and a flock of seagulls circled around her over the sculpted cedars. We wheeled home, past a pile of snow on which children were playing. It had been brought to the city as a publicity stunt and would be gone the next day. There was a full moon in the pale late-afternoon sky.

The apartment was full of people drinking tea. Armel Debru went to talk to Father in his room. I asked Marina's brother, Alexei, about the funeral services. There would be two, he said: a half-hour Mass at the house on Wednesday evening and an interment lasting an hour and a half at the Russian Orthodox cemetery on Friday morning. He explained that at least three days must pass before Olga was put in the casket, reflecting the resurrection of Christ. Having lived in America, Alexei was proud of his English. He told me a police inspector would come early Friday to seal the coffin, a law dating from the French Revolution to prevent smuggling and the switching of bodies.

I offered whisky, brought from America, and was in the kitchen setting out glasses when Marina came in and snatched the tray. "Not while Olga is in the house," she shouted.

"Too bad," I muttered to Augusto and put the glasses away. The Russians overheard the flap and seemed sympathetic and amused.

Marina's guests left about eight. Father was brought in in his wheelchair and we had dinner at the oval table in the parlor. I had trouble understanding Marina and she could not understand me. We wound up with her speaking English to me and I French to her because she could lip-read it better. She told me the family had moved five times during World War II, had twice been bombed out and had come to this apartment in 1945 from a flat near the Trocadero.

After supper Father dozed in a corner of the big room. Augusto, leaving for the night, kissed Father, Marina and Eliane, who caught him at the door. Then he came back and kissed me "to make it complete" but, laughing, declined Eliane's suggestion that he kiss Dimitri. Eliane seemed touched when I hugged her and called her "my good sister." She and Dimitri would put Father to bed after I left to go to the sanctuary of my hotel and call Jeffy in Boston.

Father was up, reading letters and telegrams, when I arrived Wednesday morning. He told me of phone calls he'd received from Rome, England and America. He and Olga had a wide circle of admirers. I felt left out.

The day passed as before: "walks" with Father in the morning and afternoon, more consultations about the future (Marina agreed that the household should go on), people coming and going, telephones ringing, naps after lunch.

As the sun was sinking over the Eiffel Tower at five, people began coming for the six o'clock Mass. There were more than a dozen of them, including all the old favorites from Olga's earlier days. These were the émigré set, more women than men, eccentric, chic and most of them penniless, including an irreverent Circassian Muslim from Romania who, Father told me, was said to have been very beautiful once. Also there were a woman from upstairs, a rabid conservative who complained that the Metro was "full of blacks and yellows," and her blonde birdlike neighbor, who appeared in a black dress and stiletto shoes with a large gold cross on her breast. My father held court in his room.

At six the Orthodox priest arrived. With his thick sandy beard and black robes, he looked distinguished and handsome. We followed him down the hall. Everyone who could crowded into the room. Father sat in a chair at the top of the stairs. Dimitri and I stood nearby with the overflow. The Mass was sung in Russian by the priest, with sung responses by Alexei and a woman I didn't know. Everyone held lighted tapers until the conclusion of the Lord's Prayer. Clouds of incense and smoke swirled over Olga's body, mingling with the scent of flowers and perfume.

When it was over, the guests went back to the big parlor. Someone told me to go to Father, who was in tears in his room with Claude Debru and Augusto. He was bowled over by the beauty of the Mass. I asked him about the passage from Ecclesiastes and he repeated it, weeping.

Soon Leila, a family friend, and others came in and I went back to the parlor for the buffet dinner of cold meat and pasta. People gathered in little groups around the room. Father sat at the table with Augusto, Eliane and Armel. Dimitri sat next to them in an armchair. The blonde lady in black went upstairs for her tiny dog, "the one who did kaka in the big chair the other day," Father said, laughing now.

I was in Father's corner with Natasha and one of the Polish twins, cat owners who had been displaced from their country home by some new Russian émigrés. We talked in French about the Mass and the coming interment. The Russian cemetery at Ste-Geneviève-des-Bois outside Paris has a special place for cats and dogs, said Natasha, who explained that there is a more famous animal cemetery in Paris, founded for a horse and dog who got their master through World War I. "The Paris graveyard has monuments and fancy plaques," she said.

"Some people go too far," sniffed the twin, who had a cat at Ste-Geneviève, as did Olga.

A Brazilian, not currently on the household team, came in with photos of a wedding in the country at Haute Borne. He had long dirty hair and unkempt clothes but nobody seemed to mind.

Nothing was scheduled for Thursday. Dimitri and I talked in the morning. He had already been to the bank to get the December and January salaries for the Brazilians. "The Credit Lyonnais said they weren't sure they could cash the check because they only bring enough for the day's transactions," said Dimitri, shocked and amused. He told me he had gone into business as an intermediary between entrepreneurs in the former Soviet Union and Westerners seeking to do business there under Perestroika. There should be no risk because the profits would come from commissions. It sounded interesting.

I wheeled Father across to the Champ de Mars. There was an ancient tree he was fond of. We sat near it and talked of the family in Boston and of his future in Paris with Marina. "She is stubborn and difficult in many ways. But we're used to each other," he said.

As we came in, the peppery concierge handed me a parcel. It was a summary of my father's will, sent express-mail from Boston. I went off to lunch with my friend Alice Furlaud in the Marais and left the will with Dimitri.

When I got back in the late afternoon, Dimitri and I called the Boston office that handled Father's money and arranged to have them send an initial $5,000 for the funeral and a monthly increase of $1,000 for the household.

I told Dimitri how grateful I was for all he was doing. "It must be hard for you. You're doing all the work and we forget that it is your mother who died," I said. Then I asked how he felt about Olga, who had left him behind when she met Father.

"The only thing I minded," he said, "was that they did not take me with them to Egypt. Except at Bénéhard, I never saw your father until they had moved to Rome. Even then, I was not invited to visit them when they first lived there." I felt paralyzed with sadness and shame. Why hadn't Father considered his stepson?

Marina was in the parlor having tea with Sergei, who used to own a house near them in the country, and Volodya, a wiry white-haired man who talked and laughed nonstop. He was Dimitri's uncle, the brother of Olga's first husband and a professor of Russian literature, still teaching at the age of eighty-one.

I sat next to Volodya at dinner and couldn't get a word in edge-wise, to the amusement of Dimitri and Eliane. But Volodya was interesting as he talked about family history and the old days at the twelfth-century castle where they all grew up. Rodony had become a school now and Volodya was scheduled to visit it sometime in the spring. We got out family albums and Dimitri got Volodya to identify forgotten aunts and uncles from the 1920s and '30s.

Father had been with Olga's body and was sorting telegrams and letters when I left for the night.

Chapter 21

Russian Funeral

I got to the flat at seven o'clock on Friday morning to find my father trying to dress himself for the funeral service. His old clothes no longer fitted him and I could only zip him halfway into a pair of black trousers that Eliane found in a closet. The undertakers came soon after that and we were told to close the doors while they carried Olga's coffin through the hall into the parlor. The house was full of people. Among them was Rukmal, who had left the household after a feud involving Father's daily sponge bath. Rukmal had responded by grabbing Father by the lips and shouting at him. Then, embarrassed, he retreated for good, or so we thought. Now, here he was again, at Olga's funeral, hugging Marina and crying. I was terribly happy that he had come back.

Suddenly the sliding doors separating the two halves of the parlor crashed open to reveal a trestle and the open casket. There was some trouble seating my father so that his chair faced Olga. The priest who had conducted the service on Wednesday, a gaunt, towering man dressed in black robes with a red and gold scarf, chanted prayers into the coffin where Olga lay like an effigy. Then he turned and took two papers from a briefcase on the couch behind him. One was the prayer of absolution, which he read and placed by Olga's left cheek, the other a small scroll, which he blessed and laid on her forehead.

The undertakers, and presumably the police inspector, then came forward with the coffin lid and there was a loud squeaking as they tightened the silver bolts all around. The doors to the flat were both open and the crowd dispersed as the coffin-bearers struggled away with the heavy load they would have to carry down five flights of stairs. I wondered if Olga would slump inside the tilted casket on the way down.

Father returned to his room where he had coffee and biscuits. Maurizio Brunori, from the lab in Rome, had missed the night plane but commandeered a friend's corporate jet and caught up with the airliner in Milan. Harry Kuiper, a Dutch colleague, had driven five hours from Holland with his wife.

With the help of Lece and Augusto, Father, Joseph and I squeezed into Bernard's car for the drive to Ste-Geneviève near the southern suburb of Fleury. Marina and others would follow in a bus. Natasha drove her own car with the twins. Bernard, an ardent Catholic with old-fashioned roots and one of my favorites, took off in a cloud of dust. He was following the priest, who drove like lightning. Through their rear window we could see Volodya at the priest's side, talking all the way.

Bernard told us that the priest, Boris Bobrinsky, supposedly got his name because his ancestor delivered Catherine the Great of an illegitimate child by Prince Orlov. The baby was presented covered in castor oil, and the name Bobrinsky (meaning castor oil) stuck with the family.

Bernard and Joseph had great fun, as we whizzed along, discussing rules in the Orthodox church: that a priest must be married, while a bishop must be celibate or widowed. "There is a saying, 'Guard it like the wife of a pope,'" said Bernard, laughing. He told us that one of Bobrinsky's sons was an engineer; the other had become a swimming instructor.

The cemetery was walled and filled with trees and flowering shrubs, unlike the bare French burial grounds. The little church with its four small domes was entirely painted inside with icons, though it was so dark and smoky you could hardly see them. There were carpets on the floor, benches along the side and a clutter of chest-high candlesticks in front of the lacquered wooden screen.

We pushed Father to the church, where Bernard and Augusto carried him in his wheelchair up the steps. In his Loden jacket and gray woolen cloak, he looked 200 years old.

A baptism was just winding down. No others in our party were there yet. Bernard joked that they had undoubtedly gone to a warmer place to sit down until it was our turn and noted that the red-haired "Russian" priest inside was undoubtedly English.

Father Bobrinsky asked Bernard whether he should say the Mass in Russian or French. They decided on French. The undertakers appeared with the trestle and coffin and laid Alexei's tribute, a huge cross of red and white carnations, on top. The female singer, left over from the baptism, passed out tapers with round cardboard shields to keep wax off one's hands. Eliane, whose mother had died four months earlier, put a lighted candle in one of the stands.

Augusto stood by my father to keep an eye on his drooping candle. I was on Father's other side, next to Jean Coursaget, the former head of nuclear medicine for the French atomic energy commission. As the church filled for Olga, Marina came in with Dimitri and stood sobbing in the crush. An old peasant barged in and joined the woman singer at the back. Bernard told us the Russian church is maintained by "these types."

Father Bobrinsky had put on the robes worn by the English priest, who now appeared in black as his assistant. The singing sounded like gods and angels. The two priests came and went between the church and the inner sanctum. Smoke filled the air until the candles were extinguished. The old peasant crashed around with a basket, collecting the candles and, evidently, money. More prayers were sung and the coffin was carried out into the damp, cold day.

Outside again, we followed the casket along the sidewalk and back into the cemetery. I spotted Madame Rado from the country. It was her husband who had carried my father back to the house when he broke his hip in the wheat field. She came up with a smile and we joined the cortege. Maurizio and Harry Kuiper from Holland were there. A lady I didn't know asked how Father was holding up. Beyond the stone wall someone was burning leaves. I wondered if it would look like this in Russia.

There were more prayers from Father Bobrinsky. Then the undertakers put iron hooks into the sides of the casket and tilted it into the hole where Olga would lie with her mother and grand-mother, and where Father would eventually join her. There was a clanking as the hooks were disengaged and Father, at the foot of the grave in his wheelchair, was offered a spoon of wet red earth to throw into the grave. Others lined up to do the same.

Before my turn came, Bernard sent word through the crowd that I should hurry to the car. Then he took off with Father in his wheel-chair and Joseph on his canes. We were the first back at the apart-ment and had no key to get in. The concierge brought a chair for Father and we were standing around in the downstairs hall when Dimitri arrived with a key to the flat.

The next hours were a blur of buffet lunch, conversations in the parlor and visits to my father in his room. The scientists were the first to leave. Maurizio caught a five o'clock train to Rome.

The ceremonies were essentially over. There would be a short memorial prayer at the big Russian church on the rue Daru on

Tuesday. And there would be a memorial Mass there forty days after Olga's death. Dimitri and Eliane were due to go back to Switzerland on Sunday. I would stay on until Wednesday.

At four o'clock I walked to the Guimet Museum, to spend an hour alone with the Asian pots and bronzes that Father so loved. What were my feelings? Not grief for Olga, who had taken Father away from us, both physically and emotionally. And for Father? Compassion surely. Love, trust, interest and amusement all mingled as I watched him weather the storm. But there was reserve too. I had come to help him over the hurdle, as you might get into the ring to calm a frightened horse. I had not come to share his grief or to take him back to Boston. I think we both knew that and it made us both sad. Cross, too, at times.

For Marina I felt genuine sympathy and concern. Enormous respect and gratitude were added to that for Dimitri. Both of them, I felt, had also been victims of Father and Olga's self-centered preoc- cupations. My father and Olga were eminent characters in their ways but I felt to love either of them was to be hurt.

When I returned in the late afternoon, Armel Debru was with Father, talking about Claude's problems at work. Eliane was in the kitchen helping to prepare dinner. In the parlor Marina was enter- taining Alexei, Natasha and Volodya. The anemones I had bought Marina were already wilting in the apartment's stifling heat.

I continued to stay at the hotel and would walk alone by the river before going to the flat. One morning I found Marina alone with her elderly crippled dog. "Now I have two to care for," she said, patting the dog. Marina told me she had looked in on Father during the night to be sure he was all right. A good augury for the future, I thought. Rukmal, who was still in Paris, came to call. I wondered if he would come back for good.

By now, Eliane had black circles under her eyes. In her quiet way, she had done as much as Dimitri to help Marina and Father through the week. As they stood on the balcony with their arms around each other, I remembered how strongly Olga had opposed their marriage.

I came in to find Father with one of the Brazilians, answering letters of condolence. I thought of how he had taught me and Jeffy not to express feelings. Now he was talking of friends and acquaintances who were "warm," wishing he could tell Olga about it all. He was fond of his caretakers because they could laugh and joke with him. I felt he got more comfort from them than from me.

The day before my departure I took my father for a long afternoon ramble past some nearby antique shops because he thought they would interest me, and along the river opposite Auteuil, where he had once been to a fancy dinner with Olga. At last I felt very close to him. We had stopped to sit on a bench near the little duck pond in the Champ de Mars when suddenly the Eiffel Tower burst into light, as if strings of flame were engulfing the huge iron grillwork soaring over our heads into the fog. I must have gasped. "They do it by magic," Father said, laughing.

It was the evening of Olga's prayer service at the rue Daru. Marina, Lydie and Augusto were preparing to leave when we got home. Father would not go because of the steps to the Russian cathedral. The table was set for two, since they all would be late getting back.

It was the only time in seven days that Father and I had been alone in the flat. And, without the guardian cats, we behaved like bad mice. I turned off the stove, turned on Augusto's lambada music and poured us each a gin and tonic. Father was in a cheerful gossipy mood.

"Alexei has a touch of the arriviste from growing up as a refugee," he said of his brother-in-law. Alexei's wife, Marishka, "is the most aristocratic of any of them. Her ancestors were the Trubetskoys, who were close to the Tsar and came down from the Dolgorukis, who founded Moscow." Alexei and Marishka, he told me, shared a house with the Princess Murat, "but, as a descendant of one of Napoleon's generals, her title doesn't count for much." The disheveled Father Bobrinsky, on the other hand, "resembles the aristocratic Tolstoy."

I asked what he thought it meant to be an aristocrat and mentioned a theory I'd read that the novels of Anthony Trollope were really about gents versus cads. "Yes," Father said. "And the gents, like Plantagenet Palliser, always lose out to the cads."

I remembered a cousin at home who maintained that a true gentleman was never rude by accident or thoughtlessness—only on purpose. "Like Will Forbes," Father observed. "And, when you think of it, like Pierre in *War and Peace.*"

We were still talking away when we heard the key in the door and the lights came on in the flat. I could hear Marina scuffing her way down the hall. She stood in the doorway to the room, smiled and waved to us. "Very, very beautiful," she said of the service and vanished. Augusto had cleared off the plates I had left on the table and came in to put Father to bed. I bent down to kiss him and told him I'd see him soon.

"Thank you for coming," Father said.

Chapter 22

Lazarus

Eighteen months after Olga's death at the age of seventy-seven, Father celebrated his own ninetieth birthday on a chilly June day at Haute Borne.

Jeff and I flew over, leaving behind a heat wave in Boston. Father was no longer able to climb up to the loft. Before her death Olga had arranged to have an addition built along the rear of the stone farmhouse. And, by 1991, Father's single bed was in a new room in back of the kitchen with a big chair and table placed next to a low casement window. A wooden ramp for his wheelchair led into the kitchen itself. Down the hall were a bathroom and a small closet-bedroom where one of "the boys" who took care of him could hear if he cried out in the night.

When he wasn't outdoors, Father spent his days in the big room at the far end of the house, his papers on a table positioned between the glass doors and a window overhung with pink roses. Plums just starting to ripen blew onto the lawn. Beyond the pines and fruit trees, beyond the fence that enclosed the garden, fields of barley and wheat showed bruises where the persistent rain had beaten the grain to the ground.

We had arrived two days before the party. Father was dozing in a stuffed chair next to the raised hearth where Rukmal or Augusto had lighted a fire. I was shocked to see that his wrists were covered with scabs halfway to his elbows where he had bitten his forearms in his sleep. Rukmal (who had returned to take care of Father) told us that once he had answered Father's nightmare cry and found him on the bed with the fingers of both hands in his mouth. In the night he dreamt that he was beset by crabs. "Recently it was a mathematical crab," Father said, laughing. Sometimes he dreamt that Olga had come to kill him.

After twenty years of Parkinson's, the drawers of my father's mental filing cabinets were falling open, the contents tumbling out in confusion. His beautiful voice had become faint. The bones in his back had crumbled away and he slept most of the time, tilted onto his right elbow, hands folded like paws beneath his chin. I was horrified that my father had come to this pass. Until now he had commanded intelligence and used it like a sword to cut through the politics of academia, to cut us children down to size, to carve his cat-like path through three marriages and into remote corners of the earth, to paint hundreds of watercolors over a couple of decades between his two almost separate scientific careers.

The room where we sat in the rain resonated with my father's past. His painting of the chateau where he had visited Olga before they were married hung next to an Italian armoire that was jumbled with books on thermodynamics and shells from beaches where he and Olga had walked together. Tribal rugs from Iran, where he had visited Will and Nan Forbes, hung on the rough-plastered walls. A stylized African bird, perhaps from his trip with Jeff to the Sudan, sat on the refectory table under the balcony leading to the sleeping loft with its tiny tub.

Marina, I knew, had always hated this room because it also contained a coffee table made from a piece of a tomb, runic letters showing through its glass top. Under a lamp in the corner was another tomb figure: a small sad-eyed Egyptian Copt holding a feather, a flower and a dagger against his bare stone chest. And by the door to the garden stood two flat wooden statues with stone eyes that once represented dead warriors at a gravesite in the Hindu Kush. Father told us that he had found them on a trip in 1956 and had had the effigies carried out of the mountains by porters who were probably half their size. I imagined the figures' eyes looking back toward the snow as they joggled over the trail. Marina was right, perhaps, to see them as omens of another death following Olga's.

But my book of photographs shows that the birthday party, when it took place two days later, was a success. Marina, hair freshly waved for the occasion, is smiling as she watches Augusto make a

Ringing in Father's ninetieth birthday at Haute Borne: at left, Olga's sister Marina, with caretakers Augusto and Rukmal. (Author photo.)

bouquet on the long green table outdoors. There is Olga's son Dimitri talking to his aunt Marishka and Dimitri's wife, Eliane, being teased by Bernard Fonlladosa. Their daughter, Marie, is knee-to-knee in conversation with Father. Alexei and Eliane look skeptical as Marishka and Dimitri get off some joke. Claude Debru, with Xenia and Natasha, from Paris. Local doctors, Thierry and Francoise, talking to Father, who is wrapped in a gray woolen cape in his wheelchair waiting for someone to cut the cake. Rukmal and Augusto sit next to Marina as Dimitri's dog, Argo, begs a crumb at Father's side.

Stanley Gill called from Colorado while Maurizio Brunori and Enrico di Cera made separate telephone calls from Rome. Even before it began my father told them the party had been a success. "It was out in the garden," I heard him say. "Many people came and it was extremely nice." Then he sat back to reread his letters and telegrams.

Later, after everyone had left or gone to bed, I sat in the big room alone. The two wooden figures by the door seemed like friendly companions. In my father's apartment in Rome they had stood on either side of a chest in the hall, guarding the house as they had once stood guard in an isolated graveyard in the Himalayas. Crudely hacked from thick boards, they were almost two-dimensional. But, with their conical hats, their arms akimbo and their white stone eyes, I imagined that they breathed quietly, dreaming of their mountain grove, seeing the flicker of timeless skies in the flicker of the fire on the hearth at Haute Borne. Today they stand guard under the eaves of a shed in my Cambridge garden.

Father has become just like these figures, I thought then. Frightening, friendly and always elusive, he belongs to the world of jungles and mountains. Like them, he has somehow escaped the measure of time. He can no longer walk, any more than the figures from the Hindu Kush. But still he can smell the smoke from the village and hear the wind through the cedar trees. On that day in June, I reflected that someday soon my father would meet death. For him it would be just like walking into a forest. Jeff and I would see the dark trees stir and feel the warm breeze, but Father would be gone.

···

But the next two years were uneventful. Then, on January 6, 1993, Jeff and I were summoned urgently to Paris. Father had been taken to the hospital with pneumonia. Alexei thought this was the end. Less alarmed, Dimitri was coming from Switzerland on the weekend. When we arrived at the little clinic in Montparnasse, silver tinsel and a silver Christmas tree still decorated the reception hall. Rukmal led us to Father's hospital room. Marina, an old knitted toque over her flying hair, sat in a chair by the window. Lifting a finger to her lips she struggled to her feet and came to greet us.

Father, now ninety-two, lay in the farther bed, mouth gaping, knees bent sideways under a white sheet. This is how he'll look when he's dead, I thought. I glanced back at Jeff. The reluctant traveler, the son who felt overlooked, he seemed to have shut himself off from the scene.

A nurse bustled in to check Father's intravenous line and the urine bag. She sent us all into the hall and, when we were allowed to return, Father was awake.

"What's that? Who's there?" he called out, his gaze turned to the window.

But when I said, "It's me, Father. And here's Jeffy. We've come to see you," he paid no attention.

"Who is it?" he cried out. "What do you want?"

My brother and I were alone with Father when the lights came on. As evening approached, he became more and more agitated. Jeff reached out to touch his foot. Father kicked out as hard as he could, both feet flailing under the loose sheet.

"No," he shouted. "I don't want it."

Lately, I had been told, Father had talked of suicide and had called Harry Kuiper, his colleague in Holland, to ask about pills. Sitting by the bed, I held his hand, rubbing my thumb over his long fingers.

"It's okay," I said over and over again. "You haven't far to go now. It's okay."

Suddenly Father reached over and tried to tear the IV out of his hand. Horrified, I held the tubes and tried to pry his fingers loose. His grip shifted to my thumb and bent it back. He was amazingly strong. He would break my finger.

"Don't," I said. "It will hurt." Did I mean hurt him or hurt me? We seemed to struggle for minutes before Father relaxed his hold.

"Father," Jeff said uncertainly. A nurse came in and straightened Father's covers.

We were both shaken as we took a bus downhill to the École Militaire and Avenue La Motte Piquet. That night I slept in the back room where three years earlier Olga had been laid out for her funeral. Jeff chose the small room next door. Neither of us wanted to occupy Father's bed, surrounded by the wheelchair and the other apparatus of his twenty years as a victim of Parkinson's.

The evening had been filled with phone calls from family and friends. Rukmal, who was now married, cooked supper with his Sri Lankan wife. They stayed for a while to talk. To my surprise even Marina agreed that Father should be allowed to die. "*Soulager mais pas prolonger*," care but don't prolong, that is what we believe, she said, glancing across the big double drawing room at the candlelit icon in the corner.

Each of us had selfish reasons for wanting this to be over, I thought. Yes, death would release Father from physical wreckage and mental distress. It would also release Jeff and me from his domination; no more summonses across the Atlantic to a hospital bed. Marina would have the flat to herself again. Rukmal and Augusto would be free to get on with their own lives. I felt guilty but I knew that I wanted my father's life to end.

Very early the next morning I was woken by a call from Father's physician. I had never met Dr. Lacant, though he had taken care of my father for almost ten years. He sounded abrupt and formal. Father seemed better. Lacant had seen him recover before. The chief of the hospital thought he could pull him through. Lacant was not sure. He was not surprised at his mental state. Violent agitation was characteristic of late-stage Parkinson's, and Father was unable to swallow at present so he was not getting his usual medicine.

Hunched over the phone, trying to marshal words in French, I felt I was babbling on. "He's had a good life. He wants to die. We don't think he should be forced to live longer. Couldn't he at least have a sedative?"

"We need not resuscitate but we cannot kill him either," said the dry voice.

The next days passed slowly. Father would seem better, then appear to lose strength. He became preoccupied with mathematics. One afternoon he talked about *A*, *B* and *C*, reached out a shaky finger and drew an *A* on my forehead. I responded by drawing letters on his forehead; he recognized *A* and *B* but not *C*. I suggested he was getting tired.

"No, I'm NOT," he said.

Later, I asked if his parched tongue bothered him. "No. Why should it?" he snapped.

Did he hurt anywhere? "No. I'm perfectly well. I want to get out of here."

I said that was up to the doctors. "Ask them when," he demanded.

I was obsessed about whether or not Father knew Jeff and me. One evening I was alone with him when Claude Debru's wife, Armel, came in to visit and began cooing over Father. He'd always attracted adoring women, pooh-poohing their possessiveness. Olga, who had been possessive too, had teased him about his acolytes. It was a liberty denied to us children and I was annoyed.

"Let's see if he can recognize this," I broke in. And, leaning in from the other side of the bed, I recited the opening lines of a Shakespeare sonnet Father had often quoted to us.

> *Like as the waves make towards the pebbled shore,*
> *So do our minutes hasten to their end . . .*

Father turned and looked at me intently. He recognized the poem, I was sure. I had his complete attention as I went on with the next lines:

> *Each changing place with that which goes before,*
> *In sequent toil all forwards do contend . . .*
> *And nothing stands but for his scythe to mow*
> > *And yet to times in hope my verse shall stand,*
> > *Praising thy worth, despite his cruel hand.*

I was thrilled. But two days later Dimitri told us that Father had talked to him about "two people who came alone." He didn't know us after all! The next morning, though, I asked Father to say my name. He pronounced it clearly. And the man standing by the window? "Why Jeffy. Jeffy!" And he did the same for Dimitri and Rukmal. He couldn't make out why I was asking.

⋯

Five days had passed and things were getting back to normal. Augusto and Rukmal resumed their job rotation. Friends came to visit Marina and took her to a memorial Mass for Olga at the Russian church in the rue Daru. Dimitri invited colleagues to the flat to discuss investments in the former Soviet Union. Jeff decided it was time for him to go home.

"There's nothing I can do," he said. "I don't speak French. I have nothing to say. You and Dimitri have spent more time with Father than I have." And then he added, "Each of you wants to do things your own way. Maybe that's why you and I don't get along."

I felt anguish at his bitterness. My brother was blaming me for doing the best I could to help, for speaking French? My God! But I did feel to blame for being intrusive, for butting in and, secretly, for taking a ghoulish interest in the pure drama that surrounded Father's illness. Father would have been interested himself. Why did Jeffy have to be so serious and so angry? But I knew that this was an old story, the bossy older sister and the sensitive younger brother.

I went with Jeffy to the travel agency and walked partway with him as he carried his small bag on foot toward the airport bus station at the Étoile. As he left, I asked him to call Father's friends in America and tell them what was going on; he promised he would. Then I turned and headed toward the hospital.

Dimitri drove back to Switzerland that afternoon and I was alone in the apartment with Marina. Because conversation with the seventy-nine-year-old Russian was so hard, I taught her to play Russian Bank. Marina won every game but the first. In bed that night I wondered if Jeffy's flight had arrived and if his wife, Margaret, had met his plane. I felt abandoned but thought of my father, alone too in his hospital bed, doing mathematics in his head and talking to ghostly scientists. The notion gave me comfort.

I stayed for another week, going to the hospital every afternoon. One day Father asked for a pencil and paper but made only faint indecipherable marks. He asked me to telephone John Edsall and I held the phone to his ear as he talked.

"I'm more or less isolated here," he told his oldest friend in Cambridge. "You know the problem. Will you come tomorrow—or even today? The result is obvious; it's pure physical chemistry . . ." I could hear Edsall's deep voice responding reassuringly on the other end of the line.

Father asked for Olga and wanted to know when she had died. "Was she cremated or buried in the old-fashioned way?" I asked which he preferred for himself. "I don't care," he said. One day when Marina came with a friend, he became very agitated again. He thought he was on a train and had to gather his packages and get off. Another time Augusto and another of the boys were with him and he was asking for his trousers so he could "get off the train." It seemed to me his mind was still set on dying.

I read poetry aloud to him and tried to follow his ideas about math and metaphysics, amazed and amused at the connections his battered mind still made. And each day he seemed stronger. He knew the old poems by heart, and now he would pick up the verses where I left off. And, when we read *The Rubaiyat*, he said, "It's the only poem Fitzgerald ever wrote, and think of its impact over time." He smiled when I told him he might get back to Haute Borne. And he told the nurses it was a joke that Jeff and I had come all this way without getting to attend the funeral. The joke was on me but I didn't mind.

One evening I went to see Dr. Lacant in his office, but my heart was no longer focused on my axe-murderer's spiel about letting Father die. And as I passed from the dark streets to the bright lights at the corner, where oysters glittered on piles of ice and waiters snapped their napkins in the glow of their restaurants, it made me happy to know that Father would be asleep at the hospital while Marina and Rukmal were waiting upstairs with dinner.

The day Augusto and Rukmal brought Father home, Marina and I went out to lunch. On the way back I made Marina stop while I bought dark French chocolates to celebrate his safe return after more than a week in the hospital. I was thinking of the time, six years earlier in 1987, when Olga and I had watched my father come back to life in the hospital near Haute Borne after the operation to replace his broken hip. After we had seen him give that small shudder and swallow after hours of stillness, I had rushed out to buy chocolates then, too. I wondered if Father would remember.

When Marina and I got to the Paris flat Father was wrapped up and in his armchair. Augusto was preparing tea and Rukmal was putting away the car. Lamplight shone on the Matisse-like wallpaper of his bedroom and my father had a bunch of papers in his hand.

"There you are," he greeted me. "What have you been doing this afternoon?" I knew it couldn't last but, by the time I left for America two days later, it was as if Father had never been away.

Chapter 23

Passing On

Father's body had already been laid out on his bed by the undertakers when Jeffy and I got to Paris for the last time. He had died in his sleep on November 4, 1995, wandering off quietly at the age of ninety-four as if for an afternoon stroll.

I left Jeffy with Dimitri, Marina and Rukmal in the big parlor at Avenue La Motte Piquet and went to see Father alone. His small room beyond the kitchen was dark except for a candle left burning on the bureau. A cold wind blew from the big casement window behind drawn velvet curtains. Marina had put flowers on the table that served as his desk. The knitted Peruvian poncho he had worn in the evenings at Haute Borne hung over the back of the chair. His framed watercolor paintings shadowed the wild wallpaper.

I looked down at the body. It was enclosed in a thick plastic bag, zipped up to the chest and partly covered with a plaid blanket. Father's arms were crossed on his chest like the arms of the little white tomb figure in the country sitting room at Haute Borne. Now, in Paris, he was dressed in a clean white shirt with his Mexican string tie fixed carefully under the collar. In the candlelight his face was very pale and still, the eyelids drawn over the eyes, his mouth closed and caved in.

Where have you gone? Where are you now? I wondered. The old voyager I had tried so hard to follow had moved on without me, leaving an empty trail behind. I reached out and laid a hand on my father's forehead. It was as cold and stiff as marble.

The funeral, like Olga's but smaller and less ceremonial, was held in the Russian Orthodox Church at Ste-Geneviève-des-Bois outside Paris. He was buried there with Olga as he had said he wanted to be. Rukmal, who had gone back to Sri Lanka with his family, flew to Paris to be at the Mass. Augusto called from Brazil. Two other "boys" from Sri Lanka would stay with Marina from now on.

As Jeffy and I flew home, we decided to have a memorial celebration in Cambridge. An Episcopal service would fit our agnostic father as well as the Russian Mass. And already I was thinking of what I would say to his American cousins and the friends who had been unable to get to France. It would be a glad message, targeted to those he'd cared about for so long.

"Now at last Father is free to do all the things he loved," I would say. "Now he can paddle kayaks with Will Forbes in the waters off Woods Hole. Now he can paint with Uncle Edward in the woods of Naushon. He can sing 'The Lover and his Lass' with Ros. Now he can chop trees at North Haven with Mother and her Cabot brothers. He can sail the Gulf of Maine from Pulpit Harbor to Roque Island and teach his children to eat sea urchins' eggs. He can walk again in the mountains outside Graz with John Edsall. He can cruise the Amazon in the *Alpha Helix* with Austen Riggs and Maurizio Brunori. He can pore over mathematical formulas in Boulder with Stan Gill and Paul Phillipson. He and Olga can sit side by side in their long chairs in the garden at Haute Borne while evening falls and the great owl floats overhead, hunting mice."

Jeffy would tell the funny story about his long walk with Father through the Sudan: How the district commissioner warned them not to cross an impassible swamp beset with mosquitoes and with savage natives at the far end. How Jeffy realized that Father would only be tantalized by this vision. And how they crossed the swamp, which was very wet and buggy, to be met by the Turkanas, who came out with bristling spears but treated them with the greatest possible hospitality in the end. Then my brother would read a recollection from Father's niece Cicely about sneaking out with Father to an art exhibit in Paris. And Jeffy would wind up with the little poem Father had made up for himself:

> On the velvet blackboard of the night
> One can sometimes read and write
> Things he cannot see in broad daylight.
> And who knows, may not the same be true
> Of the longer night that awaits us all.

The ceremony took place in Bigelow Chapel at Mount Auburn Cemetery on December 11, 1995, just as planned. The chapel, connected to the crematorium, was nice and warm. And more than sixty people came, including Ros and her husband Carl, the nurse who was taking care of Aunt Susan, now in the infirmary in Bedford, and my old partner and sometime-boss from the *Boston Globe*, Gerry O'Neill. Paul Phillipson, who spoke, and Austen Riggs, who came from Texas, joined us at a seated dinner for ten at my house the night before the service and at a buffet lunch, which lasted about three hours, afterward. I was very proud of Jeffy and felt that Father would have enjoyed it all immensely.

He would have been pleased that the chapel got its heat from the crematorium. He would have loved the fact that my neighbor led a stampede out of the lunch party, thinking cars were being towed on my street. He would have appreciated the brochure I put together, including Cicely's oil portrait of Father in his last years, which illustrated both his frailty and his enduring interest in whatever is coming next, and a photograph of him at age three blowing soap bubbles. The photo was matched with a quotation about bubbles in the river from a thirteenth-century Japanese classic called *Hojoki*. He would have missed Stan Gill, who had died of cancer in 1991 at the age of sixty, just after the publication of their book on binding and linkage. He would have been amused that among the lunch guests was a Chinese scientist from Carnegie Mellon University who was unknown to all the rest of us. And he would have been touched that among the five speakers at the service were my first cousin Powell Cabot and Will Forbes's daughter Beatrice Manz, representing not only family but also the two places in America that he loved best: North Haven and Naushon.

Looking back on my father's life, more than a decade after his death, I am still puzzled by the intense pleasure and pain he could inflict.

I admired his drive, his way of forging on and never looking back when things were going badly, as they did when he was denied the diplomatic job in Japan after his successful years at the Paris embassy, as they did again when he and Olga left the post in Cairo without a clear future, and as they did when his age and failing health forced him to leave Rome for Marina's flat in Paris.

On the other hand, like so many men of his post-Edwardian era, he led a determinedly unexamined life. His comments on psychiatry, at which I have spent so much time, seem both hurtful and absurd. I remember his writing that if one visited the dentist, why not a psychiatrist; his comment that I should only stay with the psychiatrist "if you think it does you any good"; his telling me, as a piece of secret, shameful news, that his English friend, John Kendrew, had visited a psychiatrist.

I believe his three marriages were unusually happy, each in its own way. But I remember his retrospective letter to Rosamond Forbes, his second wife, boasting that his life had "been blessed by three wives, each as different and as important in making me what I am as the primary colors are in vision." Ros seemed to think of this as affectionate and jokey. My own reaction was that my father was being totally smug and selfish. And I remember his snide remark about Jeffy's marrying someone "like one of Grandma's cooks," and the deadly way he managed to destroy or denigrate my own romances with Hugh Scott and another boyfriend, George Cornell. I can see him now, sitting on my lawn chair looking excruciatingly bored when I introduced him to George, who maddeningly didn't seem to notice.

Recently I asked Jeffy what he thought of Father as a parent. To my astonishment, my brother, who had often seemed to be treated like a foundling, said, "I think he was perfect! He taught me everything I care about in life." And Father was a wonderful teacher: interested, direct and flexible. Whether it was Jeffy asking about "tomorrow" or me trying to catch sunlight in a shoebox, whether it was making bread in North Haven or reefing a sail on Penobscot Bay, he was absolutely sure of himself and willing to explain.

I felt I could talk to my father or ask his advice about anything, from clothes to classic literature and from family feuds to strategies at work. He always gave a considered opinion, though sometimes the advice could be eccentric, as when he urged against spending money in a restaurant but approved of buying a sixteenth-century dining table, or when he joined Olga in inviting me to give up my job and travel with them around Europe, then suggested that I was being too autocratic with my staff at the newspaper.

He loved clothes, owned several very handsome English suits, and noticed what people wore but, as the Brunoris observed to me in Rome, he had no use for fashion and "used his own unfashionable style as a form of snobbism." Certainly Father was a snob; his letters were funny because he always described in minute detail the family connections of everyone he met. But I think it was more of a literary or theatrical interest than a social concern, coming partly from his voracious reading of history and partly from his own father, who seemed to feel he had nothing but his heritage to be proud of. As Father picked his way through the high tables at Cambridge University, he noted all the lions but he was also interested in many people who had made their way from nowhere. Perhaps it was a form of snobbism to be fascinated by the hippies on Boston Common and the student rioters in France and Italy. But Father genuinely loved and took a keen interest in "the boys," especially Rukmal and Augusto, who took care of him in France and were trying to make their way in the world without family, money or a particular expertise.

In this connection, Father used to ask me who I thought was "the most successful of the Cabot cousins." I assumed that he meant who had the most money or the most important job until I asked exactly what he did mean. His answer was a surprise. He said, "The one who is the most happy and fulfilled in their lives."

That answer was a revelation. It explained so much about his own life and its appeal to others. Father always did precisely as he wanted. And Father's life was one of happiness and fulfillment. Armed with the adoration of both his parents, I think he felt entitled to carve out whatever path attracted him most at any moment. He did ponder the effect of leaving Jeffy and me behind after Mother's death, but it was a turn in the road that he could not resist and, besides, the past was past. He married Ros without considering how they would manage two such different personalities or the uncertainties of two teenaged children, but their mutual affection long outlasted their unsuccessful marriage. He lived most of his adult life in Europe, and though he used to write of coming "home" and buying a country place outside Boston, it was clearly never going to happen. He was self-absorbed but his freedom was magnetic.

Ros spoke of Father's skill at drawing blood in the course of his human relationships, his odd indifference to causing pain. "He is wonderful if you are not in intimacy with him," she had once told me. Aunt Susan thought he had been "heartless" to leave a weeping Jeffy at age three to tie his shoes alone in Maine. Dimitri was deeply hurt that he was not included in Father's life until he and Olga had returned from Egypt. I was crushed when Father told me not to be "so silly" when I was joking with him and Hugh Scott after a happy picnic on the rocks off Brittany. And then there was that remark he once made to Rukmal that was so wounding that Rukmal reached out, pinched my father's lips together, told Father to "shut up" and then, embarrassed, left the household for many months, only returning for Olga's funeral. Years later, Maurizio Brunori was still dismayed by Father's curt answer to Maurizio's grieving letter about his mother's death.

Was this a streak of cruelty or a sign of unawareness? I remember how Father used to praise Jeffy's happy life with Margaret and his skill at outdoor endeavors but never complimented me on my accomplishments. Jeffy has said that Father praised me to him in the same fashion, demeaning both of us. Others have told me their parents did the same, so perhaps it was a New England tradition. Was this true, or was it like the cat who suddenly claws its owner in a kind of anguished ecstasy at having its tummy tickled?

Most of my battles with my father were fun and ended in laughter and renewed affection, like the time I pushed him off the dock in Maine and the time we fought over who should take the bath that I had drawn in Milton. Even more serious clashes, like those over

Olga's visits, were soon swept away with some phrase such as "Let's put it behind us," or with "Perhaps I am making a mountain over a molehill and your explosion in the car was only a momentary 'hot flash,' I hope so." But I had a disconcerting sense that my own needs were rarely seen or heard.

One morning in Rome recently, Maurizio's wife, Federica, asked me if I wasn't angry that Father had left us when I was thirteen and Jeffy was twelve. I realized as I answered her that of course there were times when I was angry. In the end, though, I think if he had stayed around, my father would have been a horrible parent—frustrated and ferocious, making us feel to blame for his entrapment, bored with a tame life in one place. Instead he posed a constant challenge: to survive, to take chances and to be independent.

He could be petty, as when he wrote from afar about making sure the moths weren't getting into his clothes in Milton, or when he quibbled for a year about buying me a camera. And his long letters about "his doings"—the long walks that cleared his mind, the remote travels that brought respite from the world of work, his fascination with art and culture, his gift for painting watercolors and making beautiful places to live in, his gossipy accounts of life around him—demanded that we be the keepers of his flame.

On the whole, I think he taught us well. As we celebrated Father's death with the lovely old language of the King James Bible, I reflected that Father's concern was not with doctrine but with the great dominion of ideas: the linkage of action and reaction, the ties that bind through inherited blood, the pumping of the heart that makes it possible to walk and talk, that quickens the enjoyment of high art, thoughts of distant times and people, and anticipation of events to come.

The remains of Father's ancestors lie in Mount Auburn Cemetery among the hemlock and dogwood trees. Perhaps someday Jeffy, his wife Margaret and I will be buried there, together with our mother's ashes, which have been waiting almost sixty years for burial. A marker will likely bear our names and dates. Under Mother's name it may simply say "Wife of Jeffries Wyman, 1904–1943." It will only matter to passers-by because, once we are dead, there will be no more heirs. The Wyman plot will have its final quota.

The body and the stone monument are meaningless anyhow. The spirit of the wild Cat who walked by his wild lone, the elusive parent, the peripatetic scientist and husband, the challenger and comforter has become part of the ether. There, in the thin air of memory, we will catch up and join him, part Father's offspring and part separate persons, informed by him but absolutely altered, too, by who he was.

Epilogue

Four years after my father's death in 1995, I went to Rome, hoping to meet his old friends and see his old haunts. I stayed with Maurizio and his wife, Federica. The city was buzzing with preparations for the millennium year, but the Piazza Farnese was quiet in the afternoon light. Cars had been banned from the square and the two Roman tubs stood in rosy splendor across from the palace. I went to look at the Bernini staircase that Father had so admired as he climbed to his fourth-floor apartment at number 44. The open-air market in the Campo dei Fiori had long since packed up for the day but tourists still wandered around the fountains and palaces of the Piazza Navona. I had coffee at a sidewalk cafe surrounded by motorcycles and men carrying furniture, then crossed the river and took the bus from Trastevere up the hill to the Brunoris' apartment on Monteverde.

After supper we sat and reminisced about Father. I told the Brunoris that my father's Japanese friends had repeatedly mentioned his kindness. Was it true? "I wouldn't think of 'kind' in terms of Jeffries," Federica said. Maurizio remembered writing a long and emotional letter to my father after his own mother's death and Father's responding with a brief, chilling note. Only half-joking, they said that he was a snob, referring to Mafalda, his maid, as "the servant" and deliberately wearing old clothes. Father and Olga, they concluded, bickered "like people acting in a play."

Suddenly Maurizio's mood shifted. "I thought your father was God," he said. "He had a real sense of humor and a great theoretical mind. Eraldo and I learned thermodynamics from him . . . The allosteric model was a very concrete idea, compared to the complex abstractions of relativity." Father's ideas of binding and linkage explained how enzymes enable chemical transitions to occur very fast and under ordinary conditions of life. An example, Maurizio said, is the bubbling off of hydrogen peroxide when it comes in contact with blood. The transformation might take a year in water; it occurs in a matter of seconds with blood.

The next morning I went by bus to the Regina Elena. The block-long white building fronted on a wide street, across from the university campus with its plantings of oleander and palms. It was hard to imagine the institute's scientific heyday, when Father had had a room at the top of the fourth-floor stairs overlooking the street, with Eraldo Antonini in a corner room down the hall and Maurizio one floor above. Eraldo, who in the mid-1970s drifted into research for pharmaceutical companies, died of cancer in 1983 at the age of fifty-three. Maurizio had become director of the Biochemistry Department at the University of Rome and was running its independent foundation, which has similar standing to the Institut Pasteur in Paris. Nothing remained of the days when Father worked with the team at Regina Elena.

That night the Brunoris gave a small dinner party at which I met Emilia Chiancone and Annette Alfsen, both old members of the Regina Elena group. Emilia, known as Milina, tall and aristocratic, was the daughter of a physician who directed a big pharmaceutical company in Milan. She had come to Rome in 1962 and worked on parallel paths with Eraldo. She was now studying a clam which has red blood cells that function very differently from human hemoglobin. Annette, small, feisty and French, had become the director of a research group working on the bound state of molecules at the Faculty of Medicine in Paris. We three went out to dinner the following night and gossiped about my father's taste for Milina's ricotta balls and Annette's flowering French roses.

I was still trying to learn about Father's place in molecular biology. "He had a very large view," Annette said. "He was reading Homer and understood the molecule as part of the world." Milina was more specific. "He was able," she said, "to relate structure to function and put it in a wider perspective of physiological behavior. Then he developed a mathematical theory to describe the phenomenon. Now many scientists are so specialized they can't do that."

The following day I met with Alfredo Colosimo, a biophysicist who modeled complex physical systems and believed adaptive heart rhythms are a useful response to stresses like fear. He took me to walk at the Villa Pamphili, a vast scrubby park on the edge of the city that had been one of my father's favorite haunts. Like Milina, he suggested that my father's ability to convert experimental findings into theory and then into mathematical models had led the way to further experiments and still further knowledge. "It was his philosophical approach that made him different," Alfredo said. "He took the same interest in popes and politics that he had in the aborigines. His personal curiosity about different conditions in different environments was what enabled him to make new connections in science."

Acknowledgments

Many thanks for Laura Fillmore and Protean Press, without whom the published book would not exist. And to Elizabeth Foz, an incredible, sharp-eyed, and sensitive editorial assistant; Natalya Zahn, a neighbor and artist who designed the perfect jacket; and to everyone else who worked on the book, especially Belinda Thresher, Janis Owens, Nancy Menges, and Gordon Brumm, who helped produce a beautiful book.

Index

Throughout this index, the initials *JW* refer to the third Jeffries Wyman, the father of the author and the subject of this book.

About Jeffries Wyman and His Work

"[Jeffries Wyman] took the same interest in popes and politics that he had in the aborigines. His personal curiosity about different conditions in different environments was what enabled him to make new connections in science."

> — **Alfredo Colosimo**, Professor of Biophysics,
> University of Rome

"The publication of [*Binding and Linkage* by Jeffries Wyman and Stanley J. Gill] must be regarded as a major event, and the book will surely find a place among the classics of scientific literature."

> — **Professor Serge N. Timasheff**, *Science* magazine, 1991